East Anglian Silver
1550–1750

Time which antiquates Antiquities,
and hath an art to make dust of all things,
hath yet spared these *minor* Monuments.

Sir Thomas Browne, *Hydriotaphia or Urne Buriall,*
written in Norwich, 1658

Financial support is gratefully acknowledged from:

 C&L BURMAN
Works of Art

Simon and Cathlyn Davidson

 ECCLESIASTICAL
INSURANCE YOU CAN BELIEVE IN

 GGS
CREATIVE GRAPHICS

Mason's Paper

Lycetts

 The Silver Society

Sotheby's

The Executors of the late Mrs B.C. Whiteley

The Worshipful Company of Goldsmiths

East Anglian Silver 1550–1750

Edited by Christopher Hartop

John Adamson · *Cambridge* · 2004

Published in conjunction with the exhibition *East Anglian Silver 1550–1750*
Norwich Cathedral Treasury
23rd September–17th October 2004

The text, except where credited, is by Christopher Hartop.

Copyright © 2004
Book: John Adamson
Essays: the authors
Photographs: the owners of the objects

Photographic credits appear on p. 128.

Christopher Hartop and the contributors have asserted their moral right to be identified as the authors of this work.

British Library Cataloguing in Publication Data
A catalogue record for this book is available from the British Library.

Published by John Adamson,
90 Hertford Street, Cambridge CB4 3AQ, England

First published 2004

ISBN: 0 9524322 2 6

Designed by James Shurmer

Printed on Chromomat Club 170 gsm by Saxon Group Norwich

Front Cover: Tankard, Norwich, *c.*1675–80, maker's mark of Arthur Haslewood II (no. 20)

Back cover: East Anglian decorated spoons: left to right, Norwich, 1631–2, maker's mark of Timothy Skottowe (no. 62); probably Suffolk, dated 1614 (no. 63); probably Suffolk, dated 1608 (no. 64); Woodbridge, dated 1601, maker's mark probably that of Robert Dale I (no. 67)

Inside front cover: Silversmiths at work, detail of the frontispiece from *A New Touch-Stone for Gold and Silver Wares* by William Badcock, London, 1679

Inside back cover: Paten, Norfolk, probably Norwich, dated 1674 (no. 51)

Contents

About the catalogue

The size of all objects is given in inches rounded up to the nearest ⅛ inch. The equivalent in centimeters (to one decimal place) is given in parentheses.

The following abbreviations are used: D. depth; DIAM. diameter; H. height; L. length; W. width.

Weights are given in troy ounces and pennyweights, the traditional way of weighing silverware, with grams in parentheses. There are 20 pennyweights (dwt.) in a troy ounce (oz.).

Dates are given in New Style except where indicated in the following way: 1568/9.

Provenance includes documented owners; engraved armorials are listed separately. A comma between the names of two owners indicates that the piece passed directly from the first to the second; a semi-colon indicates a gap in documentation.

Works cited under Marks:

Barrett, *Norwich Silver*:
> G. N. Barrett, *Norwich Silver and Its Marks 1565–1702*, Norwich, 1981

Grimwade:
> A. G. Grimwade, *London Goldsmiths 1697–1837, Their Marks and Lives*, rev. edn., London, 1990

Jackson:
> Sir Charles Jackson, *English Goldsmiths and Their Marks*, rev. edn., Woodbridge, 1989, with chapter on East Anglia by Geoffrey Barrett

Levine:
> G. Levine, "Norwich Goldsmiths Marks", *Norfolk Archaeology*, vol. 34, part 3 (1968), pp. 293–302. This definitive article includes photographs of virtually all recorded Norwich maker's marks.

Lynn Silver, King's Lynn:
> J. Gilchrist and B. Inglis, *Lynn Silver* (exh. cat.), King's Lynn, 1972

For other works cited in the text, see Abbreviations of sources cited, pp. 120–3.

Foreword

The Rt Hon The Earl Ferrers, PC, DL
High Steward of Norwich Cathedral

Norwich Cathedral Treasury was one of the first cathedral treasuries to be set up in the 1970s. They were set up in order to house and to display cathedral silver as well as historic plate from within their dioceses.

Norwich Cathedral Treasury came about by the generosity of the Worshipful Company of Goldsmiths. It was designed by Stefan Buzas RDI and it was opened by Mr Richard Vanderpump, who was Prime Warden of the company, in 1973.

The display in the Treasury is not static. It is not a repository of parish silver which the parishes feel that they cannot adequately look after. The items which are on display are always changing. It is thereby possible to display the most historically interesting and beautiful pieces of silver and church plate, which span five hundred years, from within the whole diocese.

It is fitting, therefore, that this loan exhibition, which is the first exhibition of its kind to show silver which has been made, not only in Norwich but in towns across the whole of the region, should take place in the Cathedral Treasury. In this diocese locally made church plate remarkably outnumbers surviving locally made secular plate from the Tudor and Stuart period by nearly 5 to 1.

Her Majesty The Queen has most graciously lent her Norwich-made beaker, which was given to her at the opening of County Hall in 1969. We are also grateful to the many churches, museums and collectors, not only in England but in the United States and Australia as well, for lending items some of which have never before been exhibited.

FERRERS

Introduction

The way silver is viewed today is quite different to the way it was regarded until as recently as a hundred years ago. While for many nowadays silver is an expensive trapping of gracious living and nothing more, in the past it was an essential element of everyday life. Not only was it a way of storing capital and displaying status in a hierarchical society, it was also prized as a durable and aseptic material with which to make vessels for eating and drinking.

Since Victorian times silver scholarship, too, has changed. The emphasis has shifted away from the old Ruskinian view of the artist/craftsman, lovingly fashioning each piece as a unique work of art, towards an image of an industry which, as early as the Middle Ages, had been one of mass production and specialization. As with all revisions, however, the pendulum is apt to swing too far and perhaps in recent years we have tended to discount the long hours of skilled labour that went into each silver object, or the close relationship between customer and craftsman. Nowhere else is this so apparent as in regional silver.

It is intended that this exhibition be seen in conjunction with the display of Norwich-made silver in Norwich Castle Museum & Art Gallery and with the Norwich civic plate now also housed in the castle keep. In selecting objects for this exhibition, the focus has been on complementing these two collections with silver made not merely in Norwich, but throughout East Anglia in order to give a survey of the region's widespread silver production. Surviving East Anglian silver is scattered in a diaspora stretching across several continents, although the quantity of surviving church plate remaining in the region, which in some cases provides important evidence for linking marks to towns or makers, is staggering. But silver made and marked in East Anglia is, of course, only part of the story: silver in use in households, guildhalls, churches and colleges of the region in the sixteenth and seventeenth centuries was a blend of items made locally, in London – and even abroad.

This catalogue is not intended to replace the pioneering work on Norwich silver by the late George Levine and the late Geoffrey Barrett, notably Barrett's 1981 book *Norwich Silver*. Levine's research in original documents was published intermittently in *Norfolk Archaeology*; Barrett's book brought together widely scattered information from these and other sources. Sheena Smith and Robin Emmerson both produced informative catalogues of silver, in 1966 and 1981 respectively. For other parts of the region, the literature has appeared spasmodically and been almost entirely confined to specialist publications with the exception of the Rev. James Gilchrist and Brand Inglis' 1972 catalogue *Lynn Silver*, which included many hitherto unpublished objects and their marks. No such work has appeared for Ipswich, Colchester or the Waveney Valley, although Henry C. Casley and, much later, Brand Inglis published research on the Gilbert family of Ipswich amd Colchester. Mary Fewster has, for the last few years, been working on a Ph.D. thesis on the goldsmiths of the entire region and it is to be hoped that her work will be published in due course.

Since its conception four years ago this project has received encouragement and help from many quarters: lenders from Britain, the United States and Australia have given the most enthusiastic response, while from the essayists, Mary Fewster, Christopher Garibaldi, Philippa Glanville, Brand Inglis, Tim Kent, Colin Ticktum and Wynyard Wilkinson, I have had the benefit of their collaboration and advice over a long period.

I should like to thank Her Majesty The Queen for graciously lending the Elizabeth Haslewood beaker. My thanks are also due to Mrs Véronique Peck for agreeing to lend the magnificent Arthur Haslewood tankard, which has not been exhibited before. Besides placing his own collection at our disposal, Colin Ticktum generously organized thirteen additional loans. I am also indebted to the incumbents and churchwardens of the parishes which have lent objects, and to numerous private collectors who wish to remain anonymous. It is the enthusiasm of many of the latter which, over many years, has fuelled so much of the research into the marks used in the region and their attribution.

I am grateful to Clare Agate, Tracey Albainy, Ellenor Alcorn, the Hon. Mr Justice Batt and Mrs Margaret Batt, David Beasley, the Hon. Mr Justice Blofeld, John and Becky Booth, John and Charmian Bourdon-Smith, Mike Boyce, Robin Buchanan-Dunlop, Robin Butler, Tim Cawkwell, Graham Chapman, Helen Clifford, Mark Cocker, David Constable, Thomas Courtauld, Cathlyn and Simon Davidson, Colin Failes, The Lord Ferrers, Sarah Foster, Michael Gettleson, Caroline de Guitaut, Eileen Goodway, Michael Hare, Jan and Michael Harrison, Mary Louise Hawkins, Nicholas Hills, Ian Irving, Faye Kalloniatis, Barry Lakey, John Larwood, Andrea Martin, Jessica Maufe, Andrew Moore, Alexandra Muir, Tessa Murdoch, Brian O'Neill, Shruti Patel, Angus Patterson, Charles and Edith Poor, Sir Hugh Roberts, Martin Roper, Trevor Rose, Timothy Schroder, Veronica Sekulese, Nicholas Shaw, Lewis Smith, Matthew Stuart-Lyon, Sue Ticktum, Kevin Tierney, Charles Truman, Nancy Valentine, Edith Welch, Harry Williams-Bulkeley and Richard S. Wolf.

Above all, my warmest appreciation goes to Nigel Bumphrey, who has been a keen supporter of the project from the outset, to Vanessa Brett, Eileen Bumphrey, Amelia Courtauld, Peter Griffin and James Shurmer, to Francesca Altman and Caroline Ellis of Norfolk Castle Museum & Art Gallery, to Dawn Amis of Norfolk County Council, and especially to John Adamson, who brought this project to fruition with his customary thoroughness and aplomb. My wife Juliet has been an inspiring partner in the project, and it is to her that I owe the greatest debt.

Fig. 1 East Anglia: a detail from *An Atlas of England and Wales*, containing 35 coloured maps drawn by Christopher Saxton, dated 1579. In Tudor and Stuart times, this was one of the wealthiest and most densely populated regions in England. *The British Library*

Silver in East Anglia[1]

Philippa Glanville

The personality of Norfolk, with its wide skies and sense of separateness, the scale of its remote churches and its regional pride, has intrigued scholars for three centuries. Norwich takes pride in its distinctive history as England's second city. It boasts the first town library outside London, the first provincial newspaper, a race meeting with silver prizes sponsored by the town from 1710 and a sturdy independence which led Thomas Havers, mayor in May 1708, to deny the Duke of Norfolk a civic entry preceded by trumpets.

An appeal to shared memory, and civic consciousness, have ensured that a few rarities have survived, such as the enamelled King John's Cup at Lynn, a relic which so intrigued Lord Burghley that he had it brought to London for examination in 1595. The Gleane Cup given to St Peter Mancroft, a mazer from Narford Hall, the Reade Salt and the striking, richly chased, Jacobean ewer and basin in the Norwich civic plate, are further survivals, demonstrating a distinct preference to preserve "curious" objects with local associations when they fell out of fashion.

For more than two centuries, since the days of Blomefield, antiquaries have pored over the rich hoard of documents about silver in East Anglia, whether *Archaeologia* printing in 1827 Sir John Fastolf's lengthy plate lists, the wills and inventories of Bury St Edmunds, or, twenty years later, the first publication of the 650 surviving Reformation church inventories. By 1884 C. R. Manning could claim with justice that these documents, combined with the lists of plate in churches, "now supply full materials for an accurate knowledge of everything relating to this part of the goldsmiths' and silversmiths' craft".

Silver for worship and silver for hospitality are the largest surviving categories of East Anglian silver, an emphasis borne out by the documents. From 137 years of marking in Norwich, the modest survival of 187 pieces of secular silver, compared to 570 pieces of church plate, shows how rapid the rate of re-cycling was. Drinking vessels and spoons pre-dominate, both personal objects and so more likely to become heirlooms, like the stoneware pot "tipped and footed with silver" left by a Suffolk gentleman to his great grandson. But focusing on the surviving marked pieces misses the extent of East Anglian rural prosperity, a picture borne out by the results of searches by the London company of goldsmiths.

Stourbridge Fair, near Cambridge, was the place to inspect "paperes of silver small wares", small pleasures like fan handles, buttons, tags or corals. Yeoman ownership of spoons, salts and cups, plus modest luxuries such as tobacco boxes, seals and bodkins, gave a modest livelihood to local silversmiths across the region, in Beccles and Bury St Edmunds, in King's Lynn and Ipswich, but such goods were easily transported far afield and particularly from London wholesalers.

Many references recapture the ostentatious, even flamboyant, displays of domestic silver enjoyed by East Anglian potentates. Famously, Sir John Fastolf's thousands of ounces of goldsmiths' work, notably his "great gilt basons of the Paris touch" were the subject of a Paston family lawsuit a generation after his death. Bishop William Brouns' lavish gift of a dinner service to his niece in 1454 was only a small part of his many bequests, including his shaving bowl, left to the priory of Norwich for ritual use. At King's Lynn the rich and diverse civic silver demonstrates how much importance was attached to the ceremonious presentation of food and drink. The crystal and silver voiding knife at King's Lynn evokes a vanished ritual of gathering the table scraps for the poor, whereas Martin Dumling's towering Nuremberg cup, almost too unwieldy for drinking toasts, reminds us that Norfolk looked across the North Sea for its trading prosperity. Goldsmiths from the Low Countries were attracted to the region, such as John Lonyson's father from Brabant.

Antiquaries are familiar with the pious generosity of the East Anglians, as in the many gifts to the altar recorded in the Black Book of Swaffham. At St Peter Mancroft at Easter, in a vivid enactment of Christ rising from the sepulchre, a silver pyx holding the Host was inserted into "an ymage of silver of our Saviour with hys woundes bleeding". The wealth of Norfolk churches is glimpsed as it disappeared into the melting pot at the Edwardian Reformation. National politics bore down on these treasured possessions. At North Elmham in 1547, was the rapid sale of church goods, and the purchase of a Protestant communion cup, intended to protect local assets, or because Gregory Cromwell was Lord of the Manor and his wife a sister of Protector Somerset?

Seven centuries of documents give inklings of the Norfolk craft. In 1141 Solomon the goldsmith briefly appears, named in a lease in St Peter Mancroft parish. Other property records around 1300 show some of Norwich's 19 goldsmiths sharing three shops "under one roof" near the market. However, the records of the assay office set up as a result of the 1564 petition for "assay and touché" have not survived and there are few inventories of shops, or bills, to extend our understanding of workshop equipment, or of the balance of stock between jewellery, small wares and larger commissioned pieces.

Archives can only hint at the complex reality of the trade. With goldsmiths' work, as with pewter, and later watchmaking, networks ran from London to the regional fairs, notably Stourbridge, on the outskirts of Cambridge, and between Norwich retailers and London, where both components and finished goods could be supplied. Questions arise about technical skills such as refining. Between 1547 and 1552, when so many parishes dutifully converted many thousands of ounces of altar plate into cash, who handled the resulting bullion? St Peter Mancroft sold off 857 ounces and Alderman Felix Puttock bought 316 ounces at five shillings the ounce from St Andrew's in Norwich in 1549.

Enamelling and casting are both techniques demanding specific knowledge. Were the finial or the coats of arms on the Reade Salt in fact produced in a Norwich workshop? Or, as indicated by a bequest to that city of a pounced cup "of London touch" in the will of Peter Peterson, were the leading goldsmiths in the region also acting as retailers for London goods, and organising commissions? Plate knows no boundaries and can travel far from its place of making. The focus in the past century and a half on makers' marks has obscured the reality of a prosperous many-layered market, in which goldsmiths across England were retailers. The elegant script engraved on the Colkirk cup and paten, supplied by Elizabeth Haslewood in 1697–8, hints at the sophistication and prosperity of late Stuart Norwich. The goldsmith

Thomas Havers, free in 1674, was a landed gentleman, a receiver of letters and a prominent citizen. He clearly was not active at a workbench. The city's local goldsmithing business was too slight to sustain an assay office after 1700. In the lists of freemen, the term goldsmith rarely occurs: for example, between 1715 and 1752 only four were admitted. As with the Norwich watchmakers, the reality was that they retailed, repaired and took commissions.

In the mid 1690s, when Norwich successfully petitioned to have a mint again, this must have involved the local silversmiths, if only as receivers of old plate brought in for conversion to coin by their regional customers. Several hundred poundsworth of small coin was produced, and the melting may account for the shortage of locally marked plate of the late seventeenth century. Unlike Chester or Exeter, cities of similar size in their regions but further from London, Norwich, being close to busy trade routes, did not sustain a local industry after 1700. The term goldsmith now designated a banker, a jeweller or supplier of financial services, men such as Charles Weston, a brewer who set up the first provincial bank in 1756, or Sir John Harrison Yallop, mayor in 1815 and 1831, whose shop at the north corner of Davy Place on the Walk sold government lottery tickets.

Paradoxically, although Norwich was England's second city until the eighteenth century, and attracted silversmiths from Scotland, France and Germany, the small numbers in the trade limited their civic role. Metalworkers were only six per cent of the Norwich trades around 1300. The *Liber Albus* of 1426 listed five goldsmiths as new freemen out of 120. Between 1512 and 1749, 7,000 apprentices were enrolled, but only 35 were indentured to goldsmiths.

This exhibition and catalogue is the fruit of recent and ongoing research. Together with the symposium *Silver in East Anglia* held in October 2004, an innovative collaboration between the Castle Museum, the University of East Anglia and the Silver Society and one drawing on the strengths of each, it has triggered a reassessment of a region rich both in antiquarian traditions and in surviving objects.

1   Thanks are due to Gordon Glanville for his systematic exploration of East Anglian sources to support this essay.

Goldsmiths in Norfolk and Suffolk, 1500–1750

Mary Fewster

Between 1500 and 1750 over two hundred goldsmiths can be traced working in East Anglia. They are found in the main urban centres of Norwich, Ipswich, Bury St Edmunds, King's Lynn and Great Yarmouth, and also in some market towns, notably Beccles, Bungay and Harleston. This exhibition includes pieces which can be identified with each of these areas, either definitely or speculatively through distribution patterns. The presence of goldsmiths can be explained by considering the administrative and trading foci of the region.

East Anglia was a wealthy area in the sixteenth and seventeenth centuries. By 1515 Suffolk was four-to-five times wealthier than it had been in 1334, and Norfolk was three-to-four times richer.[1] Ranking of provincial towns by taxable wealth in 1524–5 shows the five main East Anglian urban centres in the top eighteen towns. The combination of farming, the cloth industry, proximity to the sea and to the continent in terms of trade, navigable rivers and reasonable conditions for travel by road resulted in a large and mobile population and consequently in several large towns providing a wide range of goods and services, and a large number of market towns serving their local areas or providing facilities for travellers.

The populous nature and the wealth of East Anglia resulted in a complex network of trade routes and trading centres in Norfolk and Suffolk. Writing of Suffolk, Diarmaid MacCulloch pointed out the importance of rivers both in defining external boundaries and internal communication within the county,[2] and a similar case could be made, to a large extent, for Norfolk. However, between Norfolk and Suffolk the real "trade boundary" is not the river Waveney, which is the county boundary, but further south towards Halesworth.

The road patterns draw people in the Waveney valley to shop in Norwich today, and the distribution of Norwich communion cups in the northern deaneries of Suffolk show that this was the case four hundred years ago.

If direct road travel was a factor in establishing trading patterns, so was the need to reach certain centres for the purposes of attending civil and ecclesiastical courts and paying taxes. Norwich, as the provincial capital and one of the major cities of the country, provided commercial and industrial opportunities which brought trade and custom from a wide area of East Anglia.[3] As the centre of a large diocese and a provincial capital, it benefited from a long-established pattern of movement for official purposes such as church courts, assizes and taxation, while the importance of the cloth trade encouraged production and trading activities. King's Lynn and Yarmouth, the two other major towns in Norfolk, were important ports, each with established hinterlands and fairs which drew custom from a wider area.

In Suffolk, trading patterns were influenced by both geography and administrative patterns. The county administration was divided into four parts: the liberty of St Edmund, the liberty of St Audrey, a small liberty of the Duke of Norfolk in the north of the county, and the Geldable, which had two foci, in north Suffolk and around Ipswich, connected by a corridor running through the centre of the county.[4] The liberty of St Edmund was centred on Bury St Edmunds, providing a capital for west Suffolk, as it does today; the liberty of St Audrey, retained by the Dean and Chapter of Ely after the Reformation, was administered by their stewards resident in east Suffolk, and by the sixteenth century was administered from Woodbridge.[5] The remaining sector, the Geldable, which was the only part of Suffolk to pay its tax to the king, had its capital in Ipswich, which was in the south-eastern corner of the county and therefore not conveniently placed. Not surprisingly, the eastern side of the county had far less of a sense of unity than west Suffolk, and this can be seen in the complex patterns of its road networks. Two major county towns emerged: Ipswich and Bury St Edmunds. Ipswich was the centre for the Geldable in the east, while Bury St Edmunds was the centre of the Liberty of St Edmund in the west of the county. The centre for the third unit, the

Liberty of St Audry, was variously at Wickham Market, Melton, and by about 1578, when its shire hall was built, at Woodbridge.[6] The Duke of Norfolk's Liberty had manors in sixteen parishes, including Bungay.[7] Quarter sessions in Suffolk might therefore be held in Beccles, Woodbridge, Ipswich and Bury. In the south-west of the county Sudbury served south-west Suffolk and the northern part of Essex.

One of the most important cross-county routes ran from Bury St Edmunds to the coast at Yarmouth, through the towns of the Waveney valley. In this border country, away from the orbit of the major centres, the market towns seem to have acquired added importance for the local yeomanry and minor gentry, and provided services for travelling trade. There was also river traffic: in the sixteenth century improvements to the Waveney enabled goods to be brought up from Yarmouth to Bungay and, if Swinden's history of Great Yarmouth is to be believed, the river was navigable to Weybread, upstream of Harleston.[8] Goldsmiths can be traced at both Bungay and Beccles, as well as at Harleston. The last of these grew up as a fairstead in the corner of the parish of Redenhall,[9] but "with so many watercourses, tracks and roads converging upon it, Harleston was by nature marked out for a distributing centre and so struggled out of its eclipsed position of being only a part of Redenhall parish."[10] Reference to both goldsmiths and pewterers at Harleston indicate greater trading importance than its origins and continuing parochial status as a chapelry of Redenhall would justify; and this is underlined by the fact that Norwich men sold corn at its market.[11]

As the regional capital and the centre of the diocese, Norwich attracted, and could sustain, a larger number of goldsmiths than any other town in East Anglia, with six to eight workshops operating at any time during most of the period. A guild of goldsmiths existed from the fourteenth century. Goldsmiths took leading roles in the hierarchy of the Company of St George.[12] At the beginning of the sixteenth century, therefore, the mechanism of craft control was long established, and the leading goldsmiths of the early sixteenth century were powerful and wealthy men prepared to act together to try to protect their trade from interference from the London company of goldsmiths. Despite this they did not take advantage of the grant of the right to assay, given to Norwich in 1423 as well as to the cities of Bristol, Coventry, Lincoln, Newcastle-upon-Tyne, Salisbury and York. This privilege enabled the goldsmiths of Norwich to possess

Fig. 2 The Reade Salt, silver-gilt, Norwich, 1568–9, maker's mark of William Cobbold (*c*.1530–1585/6). Peter Reade was a mercer of Norwich, who in his early life had served abroad as a mercenary. At the siege of Tunis he had been knighted by Charles V. In 1568 he left "the Mayor, Shreves, Cittizens in remembrance of my good will £20 wch they shall put in som peace of plate beying eyther a salte or a boll with a cover, and my arms to be set upon the same to remayne and serve the mayor and successors for ever". It was re-gilt by Nathaniel Roe I in 1734. *The Corporation of Norwich*

Fig. 3 Communion cup of St Margaret's, Norwich, silver, parcel-gilt, Norwich, 1567–8, maker's mark a sun in splendour for Peter Peterson I (fl. 1554–1603); also struck with another maker's mark of a trefoil slipped (see pp. 35–6). This cup links the sun mark to Peterson (see fig. 4). *Norwich Castle Museum & Art Gallery*

their own sterling mark and assay their own plate. But it was not until the 1560s, with the general conversion of the massing chalice to the communion cup, that the Norwich goldsmiths felt the need to re-establish their right to assay, being warned by the London company of goldsmiths of the possible problems of substandard working caused by the overwhelming demand for the re-making of chalices.

The senior wardens of the Norwich goldsmiths' company had the authority to assay plate, to require each goldsmith to stamp his mark on items previously hallmarked, to search the shops and houses of working goldsmiths for defective wares, and to seize and break up any works of inferior silver. It is interesting that the additional power and control that this gave to the wardens is vested in only three men in the key years 1564 to 1568: William Cobbold, William Rogers and

Peter Peterson.[13] They were no doubt the leading goldsmiths of the time. The quality of Cobbold's work is shown in the Reade Salt, generally acknowledged as one of the finest pieces of provincial civic plate, and the quantity of his work which survives – 116 pieces of church plate alone survive in Norfolk and Suffolk churches – shows both that he was able to attract custom and to operate a scale of business to satisfy this demand. Peter Peterson was already taking a prominent part in civic affairs and served as chamberlain from 1570 to 1579. He was an established master craftsman with Cobbold's son as one of his apprentices, although the surviving work is not exceptional – perhaps because his civic duties caused him to leave much of it to journeymen. He was, though, familiar with the London company. He was sworn as a member of it in London in 1545, and therefore may have been working there at the time, which would explain why he did not become free in Norwich until 1553, at the age of 35. William Rogers had been apprenticed to a London master, Jasper Palmer,[14] became a freeman of the company of London goldsmiths, and worked there for some time before becoming free by purchase in Norwich in 1557. His mark has not been identified, but Colin Ticktum has made a suggestion on page 35. Rogers must have been a major maker and was familiar with the standards and fashions of the capital. In addition to these major figures, a fourth goldsmith, George Fenne, "Dutch George", may also have had the expertise to undertake the task of assaying. He appeared in the city as a qualified goldsmith and became free in 1567. Interestingly, the zigzag assay gouge found on most of the marked plate of this period has been considered to have similarities to Dutch styles of assaying.[15]

Following the surge of activity at the time of the making of the communion cups, there is no record of the organization

Fig. 4 The churchwardens' accounts for St Margaret record under 1565: "pd. To Pet' Peterson, ye Goldesmyth, for making ye communion cuppe, for every owne wourken vj*d*. Sm. xij owc and di vj*s*. Iij*d* … It. Paid more to him for iij qrtrs of a ownc sylver iiij*d*" The cup is marked with the sun in splendour. Under 1568 the accounts record: "It. Pd. For amendinge ye communion cuppe, and for makinge ye cover, ii*s*", but they do not record the name of this goldsmith whose mark, the trefoil, is discussed on pp. 35–6. *Norfolk Record Office MF897*

towards the end of the century. As there were still powerful and wealthy goldsmiths, it may be that for some years the fault lay in the mayor's court records rather than in the formalities of the guild. However, the city's regulation of the craft was strengthened through a general reform of the craft guilds in 1622. The crafts were grouped to form twelve companies, each headed by one of the more prestigious crafts. The goldsmiths headed the Sixth Grand Company, which also contained "Ironmongers, Smithes, Sadlers, Pewterers, Brasyers, Glasyers, Cutlers, Plomers, Clockmakers, and Bellfounders", and was placed under the supervision of the alderman of the ward of East Wymer.

The Norwich company of goldsmiths appears to have reacted swiftly, again suggesting that its organization might have been operating efficiently. It presented the names of its wardens in 1622, and then presented its laws to the Norwich Assembly for enactment in 1624.[16] These laws reaffirmed the earlier ordinances in respect of the control of apprenticeship and foreign workers, the making of searches and the assaying and marking of work. They also give valuable detail of the way the craft community operated.

From time to time the Mayor's Court Books for the period record that, in addition to the wardens and the beadle, there was the yearly appointment of a "saymaster" or assay master, who was clearly responsible for the expert task of assaying and marking the plate. Edward Wright's appointment as saymaster was first recorded in 1624, yearly to 1629 and then again in 1635.[17] The new regulations also instituted an additional mark of the crowned rose, as specified in the Saymaster's Oath, which was recorded in the Mayor's Court Book.[18]

The civic and religious turmoil which Norwich experienced between 1642 and 1688[19] is no doubt the best explanation for the failure of the Norwich goldsmiths to revive their company organization after the Civil War. Goldsmiths worked and prospered in these years – both church and secular plate exist marked by Norwich goldsmiths with their own marks and with versions of the town or the crowned rose marks, but clearly there was no "official" marking or date letter sequence.[20] The ending of this period of "chronic constitutional, political, and religious instability"[21] was probably the spur to a re-establishment of a formal structure and new dating series, even if the basic business of the company – the overseeing of apprenticeship and the communal activity – might have been continuing unabated.[22]

This final period of the regulation of the craft was beset with problems. Ten years after the re-introduction of a full set of marks the Britannia Act of 1697 was passed, raising the standard of silver from 92½ per cent to 95 per cent. This prevented the use of coin and required the goldsmiths to purchase ingots. The act introduced a new stamp of Britannia, but also prohibited the stamping of Britannia silver other than through the London Assay Office. The future of the Norwich Assay, and therefore the status of its goldsmiths, were in doubt. The provincial goldsmiths reacted with fury, and sent petitions to Parliament.[23] This achieved the desired result, and a bill for appointing wardens and assay masters for the provincial assay offices began its progress through Parliament on 29th March, 1701.

On 1st July, 1702, Robert Harsonge (or Hartstrong) was sworn as "assayer of gold and silver to the Company of Goldsmiths of this City."[24] The stage seemed set for the healthy continuation of the craft into the eighteenth century, so it is surprising that only three pieces stamped with the Britannia mark are known, and all these bear the date letter A for 1702. The maker's mark in each case is HA. Under the Britannia Act the maker's mark had to be the first two letters of the goldsmith's surname, but unfortunately four goldsmiths had names beginning with these two letters: Havers, Harsonge, Harwood and Haslewood. The apparently abrupt end to the Norwich Assay cannot be because of the death of Harsonge. He voted in the 1714 election, and was alive at the time of his son's death in 1717.

In contrast to Norwich, none of the other main centres in East Anglia had a right to assay, and none seem to have had a company of goldsmiths. This is probably because of the small numbers of craftsmen involved at any one time – probably one to three workshops. Only in Ipswich do goldsmiths, as a body, seem to have taken part in civic ceremonies. Here and in the other towns the corporation and a guild merchant dealt with the formalities of apprenticeship and freedom, and any disputes regarding business matters.

As suppliers of luxury goods and needing to show their wares, the goldsmiths were found in central areas, and seem to have favoured a thoroughfare site. In Norwich, they settled in the wealthy central parishes of St Peter Mancroft, St Andrew, and St Michael at Plea. Originally they occupied part of the north side of the Market Place in an area from Holtor [Dove Lane] to Rackeythe [later Rackey Lane and then Swan Lane], called in the thirteenth century "Vicus de

Fig. 5 Tankard, silver, Norwich, 1702–3, maker's mark HA for Robert Harsong, Thomas Havers, Arthur Haslewood III or Robert Harwood. One of only three recorded Norwich pieces struck with Britannia standard marks. *Christie's*

Aurifabria" and from 1372 "Le Goldsmytherowe".[25] John Tesmond, one of the few goldsmiths to become mayor,[26] was recorded as living in this area in the 1580s.[27] His journeymen at that time subsequently became wealthy goldsmiths in their own right: John Gray and Nicholas Wharlowe, both of whom later had premises further along the street in St Andrew's parish. In the seventeenth century Elias Browne, who became Sheriff in 1660, and in the eighteenth century Thomas Havers, one of the last active goldsmiths and mayor in 1708, had their houses and premises in the Market Place. Between 1717 and about 1795, so did Nathaniel Roe and his son, also Nathaniel. A print of 1850 shows Rossi's shop in this traditional area, probably occupying the same premises as had earlier craftsmen.

Other goldsmiths had their houses and premises in the eastward continuation of this row, of which parts were at various times called Hosiergate, Cutler Row, Cockey Lane, and London Lane. Here in the sixteenth century were William Cobbold, William Rogers, Peter Peterson, John Basyngham, probably John Gray, and Nicholas and

Valentine Isborne. In the eighteenth century the Haslewoods' workshop was in the western part of the street. The road from here led down to the cathedral, opposite which goldsmiths' properties can be identified, along the west side of Tombland – the old Saxon market place and the site of the Tombland Fair – and for a while some, such as Thomas Worcester, Richard Herys and Thomas Bere, had workshops in the Great Court of the Cathedral Priory itself, between the west end of the Cathedral and the Erpingham Gate.[28]

In Ipswich, goldsmiths were also found only in a small area of the commercial centre of the town, mainly in the parish of St Lawrence. Matthew Gerard or Garrard, Hertyk Crewling and John Sheytt all requested burial in St Lawrence's,[29] as did Jefferye Gilbert,[30] the first of the family of Ipswich goldsmiths who would seem to have dominated the craft throughout the sixteenth century. A property transaction in 1569 involving Jefferye Gilbert and his fourth wife Katherine referred to properties including two shops opposite the Fishmarket, as well as the goldsmith's workshop in the occupation of Jefferye Gilbert and Katherine his wife.[31] At least one eighteenth-century goldsmith lived and worked in the same parish. The premises of most of the major Bury St Edmunds goldsmiths were on Cooke Row. Evidence for this can be found in deeds and in the will of one of the most prominent Bury goldsmiths of the sixteenth century, Erasmus Cooke.[32] The street was the main thoroughfare from the Market Place to the gates of the Abbey, an identical situation to that of London Street in Norwich. More evidence of sixteenth-century goldsmiths in Cooke Row is shown in the will of Margaret Oliver alias Stone, the widow of Robert Stone, who died in 1577. She referred to "my shope wherin is wroughte and shewed goldsmythes ware situate in the Cooke Row nigh unto the Whighte Lyon."[33] This site can be identified in modern-day Abbeygate Street – a good corner site currently occupied by a jeweller.

In King's Lynn, too, goldsmiths' premises were mostly along the main street connecting the Tuesday and Saturday Market Places. This street, known at different times as Cook Row, Mercer Row and Bridgegate (or Briggate) Street, was clearly a good site for business premises, and in 1623 among the list of Quitrents a tenement at the point where Cook Row became Mercer Row was held by James Wilcocke,[34] who became free by purchase in 1593.[35] In Baxter Row Francis Cobbe held a property[36] which could have been his workshop premises, and probably his house. From the junction of Cook Row and Mercer Row a cross street called the Grassmarket led east, and further on became Damgate. Thomas Bolden, who became free by purchase in 1556/7,[37] held tenements, including his premises, in Damgate in 1568, and these, in separate occupation, were referred to in 1623 as "sometime Bolden's".[38]

The position of goldsmiths' premises in the smaller centres is more difficult to discover, but it is reasonable to expect them to have been in the market-place or main shopping street. Thomas Bathcome of Woodbridge left to his wife a tenement in the Thoroughfare, which was probably his shop and house.[39] The Thoroughfare is still the main shopping street.

One benefit of studying East Anglia as a whole is that for the first time due consideration can be given to the movement of goldsmiths. Even in the second half of the sixteenth century, when the remaking of the communion plate and the increased prosperity of the period resulted in an increase in the number of major goldsmiths' businesses in Norwich, there were more entrants to the craft than the trade of the city could accommodate. Less successful goldsmiths, or newly admitted freemen, were tempted to move on to areas where there were fewer established goldsmiths and where there was more opportunity for business or advancement.

Thomas Buttell became a freeman of Norwich by purchase in 1565, having arrived in Norwich prior to 1563, when his son John was baptized in St Andrew's church.[40] Perhaps he worked as a journeyman for one of the Norwich goldsmiths, but seized the opportunity to set up independently when the order came to remake the communion cups. Fifty-one pieces of plate marked with his mark (the flat fish) and the Norwich date mark for 1567 are extant in Norfolk churches. The following year he left for Cambridge, obviously in anticipation of the conversion of chalices in the Ely diocese. During a visit to Stourbridge Fair by the wardens of the London company of goldsmiths in 1569 they "brake and defaced viij communion cuppes with iiij covers, all white, found in the handes of Th. Buttell of Norwich then working in Cambridge."[41] There are 31 extant pieces with his mark in Cambridgeshire churches, and with a further three in Huntingdonshire and five in Northamptonshire.[42] He was also the most considerable provincial goldsmith refashioning plate in the Peterborough diocese.

Those who moved from Norwich were, like Buttell, newly free, and tended to move north or west rather than towards London. King's Lynn seems to have been a magnet for young

craftsmen, and the majority of goldsmiths there became free by purchase. Richard Waterman, apprenticed to William Cobbold and free in 1560, remained in Norwich until the mid-1560s (he lived in St Andrew's parish and his children were baptized there in 1563 and 1564), but in 1567 became free of King's Lynn by purchase.[43] Therefore, unlike Buttell, he did not stay in Norwich during the major period of refashioning of plate, but perhaps saw the possibilities of work in the west of the county. His mark is unknown, and therefore it is impossible to suggest how much work he did in that area.

The seventeenth-century goldsmith William Howlett became free in 1628, having been apprenticed to John Howlett, his father or uncle, and almost immediately left for King's Lynn, becoming free by purchase in 1629. The mark attributed to him (H over W) is found on cups at Middleton (1632), Weasenham (1633, no. 88) and Barmer (1635), all in

Fig. 6 Communion cup of St Peter, Repps, silver, Norwich, 1567–8, maker's mark of Thomas Buttell (fl. *c.*1564 – after 1570). The mark, a flat fish or butt, is a pun on his name. *The Worshipful Company of Goldsmiths*

west Norfolk, as well as on a small cup in Lincoln Cathedral dated 1642.[44] He was still in King's Lynn, and working, in 1663, aged about 60, when he gave evidence at an enquiry.[45]

Although King's Lynn could be the destination for young Norwich goldsmiths, the market opportunities there were clearly limited, and one King's Lynn goldsmith can be traced who decided to move further north into Lincolnshire. Edward Nodale or Noddall was apprenticed in Lynn to Francis Cobbe, and became free in 1623. He died in Boston in 1636–7[46] and it is suggested that he was the maker of the Gosberton Chalice.[47]

Limitations on the numbers of goldsmiths able to be sustained in a town like King's Lynn would lead to this fluidity of movement. This appears to be the case with William Letsham or Letsam. He appeared in the Lynn records in 1587, becoming free by purchase. He seems to have originated in Bury St Edmunds, having been brought up by Margaret Oliver alias Stone. Margaret died in 1577, leaving Letsham a legacy of 40 shillings in her will, and he would therefore have been a young, qualified goldsmith when he arrived in Lynn. As there is no further reference to him there, was he the William Letsham, goldsmith, who died in the parish of St Giles without Cripplegate in London in 1626?[48] The evidence of William Howlett shows that goldsmiths might still be working in their late sixties.

Established provincial goldsmiths seldom seem to have moved. One exception was Lawrence Gilbert, who returned to Ipswich from Colchester on the death of his father and seems to have taken over at least part of the business. Despite the position of Norwich in the ranking of provincial towns, it does not seem to have encouraged qualified goldsmiths to move from other, smaller or less important centres. Only fourteen Norwich goldsmiths became free by purchase. Of these, six were Strangers, immigrants from the Low Countries, all but one of whom probably arrived as skilled craftsmen; the sixth, Zacharias Shulte, would seem to have been the son of Zachary Shulte and was most likely apprenticed to his father but born before his father's freedom in 1548.[49] Two others, William Kettleburgh and William Rogers, can definitely be traced as from Norfolk families and apprenticed in London, and it is likely, from the names, that most of the remaining six also originated in Norfolk. Immigrant goldsmiths can also be traced in both Ipswich and King's Lynn, both ports being good points of entry to the country, and with close links with the Low Countries. In

Ipswich, Martyn Denys, William Myles and the goldsmith called Adrian or Andrew were immigrants from the continent. Of the three, only Myles appears in any other record, and like other first generation "strangers" they were doubtless under restrictions as to the work that they could do.[50]

In the seventeenth century there is less indication of mobility. Brooks suggests that population stagnation and high mortality in the later seventeenth century reduced the pressure from rural apprentices and encouraged "self recruitment" through the apprenticeship of sons.[51] The "two-generation" workshop had always been a feature of the craft, for example, William and Matthew Cobbold, the two John Basynghams (possibly uncle and nephew), and Nathaniel Roe I and II. Rarely, either because of a lack of sons or attempts at upward mobility, did longer dynasties appear. The three Chestens in Beccles (Hamond, John and Richard) would seem to be one case, although little is known about them. The Gilbert family continued for over a century in Ipswich, probably in the same workshop, from Jefferye Gilbert, free in 1530 to his grandson Jefferye, probably still working in 1645. The best documented family is that of the Haslewoods of Norwich, who were working from the freedom of Arthur Haslewood I in 1625 to the death of Arthur Haslewood III in 1740. Within this dynasty is one of the cases of a widow continuing to run the workshop after the death of her husband. Elizabeth Haslewood was the widow of Arthur Haslewood II, and carried on his business, marking with her own mark of EH under an openheaded crown. No doubt she employed journeymen goldsmiths, one being Lionel Girling, whose mark appears with hers, but it is not known whether she was skilled as a goldsmith. In 1685 she regilded the City Sword (not Mace, as in Barrett) at the cost of 42s. 6d.[52] and in 1686 was fined 13s. 6d. by the London goldsmiths' company searchers for substandard silver. She died in 1715 and lies buried by her husband in the south aisle of St Andrews.

The death of her son, Arthur Haslewood III, seems to signal an end to the era of the working master goldsmiths. Throughout the seventeenth and into the eighteenth century the line between clockmakers or watchmakers and goldsmiths became increasingly blurred. For example, Elias Browne was free as a clockmaker, and Robert Harsonge described himself variously as a clockmaker and a watchmaker. In Ipswich, Francis Colman and Thomas Holborough I and II were goldsmiths, watch and clock-makers. Others became mainly jewellers, or would appear, like Nathaniel Roe I, to have been retailers of luxury goods, including tea, coffee, china and snuff.[53] His son, Nathaniel Roe II, was the last goldsmith to become mayor, in 1777.

1 Schofield, pp. 508–9

2 MacCulloch, pp. 13, 19.

3 Dymond, p. 166, refers to the calculation based on thirteenth century surnames that at that time Norwich had drawn in people from at least 400 villages in Norfolk and a further sixty in Suffolk. These must reflect to some extent the area of the Norwich hinterland.

4 See MacCulloch, pp. 21–2.

5 MacCulloch, pp. 13, 19; Scarfe, plate 29.

6 Scarfe, pp. 40–41.

7 White, pp. 4–5.

8 Best, p. 21.

9 Dymond, p. 153.

10 Granville Baker, p. 96.

11 Minutes of the Norwich Court of Mayoralty 1630–31, Norfolk Record Society vol. 15 1942, p. 120.

12 This religious fraternity was conjoined with the Corporation in 1452 to prevent factional rivalry between the city's rulers. It continued to exercise control over the membership of the Corporation until the "honourable tyrannical company" was dissolved in 1731–2.

13 The names of the elected wardens of each craft were recorded in the Mayor's Court Book each year, except for a brief hiatus during the Reformation period, when the guilds were abandoning their role as religious fraternities and were unsure of their status. However, the Mayor soon made it clear that the swearing-in of wardens, and the supervision of craft practices, was to resume, and the lists of wardens began again in 1551, although the goldsmiths do not seem to have presented their wardens before 1564 (Barrett, *Norwich Silver*, pp. 8, 20) The sequence of wardens during the years 1564–68 was:
     1564–5 William Cobbold and William Rogers
     1565–6 Peter Peterson I and William Rogers
     1566–7 Peter Peterson I and William Cobbold
     1567–8 William Cobbold and William Rogers
   (Barrett, *Norwich Silver*, p. 20).

14 Ibid., p. 92.

15 This observation appears in a note by Cecil Gibson following a NADFAS meeting on Norwich silver in 1994 and has been confirmed by Christopher Hartop (see p. 25) and others.

16 These laws have been transcribed in *Norfolk Archaeology*, vol. 24, pp. 211–21.

17 Barrett, *Norwich Silver*, p. 29. Barrett points out that Wright's son, also Edward, became free in 1649, and was the master of Robert Harsonge, who was appointed assay master in 1702. From this he suggests that a continuous run of office was held by these three men.

18 Barrett, *Norwich Silver*, p. 29, transcribes the oath in full. The crowned rose mark was clearly intended to be equivalent of the lion passant, struck on London silver since the 1530s, which had become the sterling standard mark.

19 See Evans, chapters V–VII for a detailed analysis of the period.

20 Among goldsmiths active in this period were Elias Browne, who became sheriff in 1660, John Leverington, who married Browne's widow, was sheriff in 1672 and became alderman in 1688, Robert Osborne, Thomas Havers, who became mayor in 1708, and the Haslewood family.

21 Evans, p. 318.

22 Philip Howard, "Norwich Craftsmen in Wood 1550–1750" (M.Phil. thesis, UEA, 2000), p. 143, notes a similar change from the mid 17th century in the guild organization of the woodworkers. Dealing with much larger numbers, he sees it as a change from a fraternity to domination by a few large workshops. The small numbers and specialist function of the goldsmiths seem to have created this hierarchy in the sixteenth century. If anything, the loosening of the guild structure would have given more opportunities for the small, independent craftsmen.

23 Barrett, *Norwich Silver*, p. 47, gives the entry in the *Journal of the House of Commons* relating to the petition from Norwich.

24 Ibid., p. 48.

25 Kirkpatrick, p. 26.

26 *An Index to Norwich City Officers*, Norfolk Record Society, vol. LII, p. 151. He was mayor in 1601.

27 Norwich City Archives, case 13a.

28 NRO, DCN 1/4/104-116.

29 NRO, NCC wills 139–140 Spurling; NCC wills 166 Grundisburgh; Probate Records of the Archdeaconry of Suffolk R8/162.

30 ESRO, IC/AA1/25/194.

31 Redstone, *Extracts from Ipswich Borough Records*, MS in Ipswich Record Office, vol. 12, p. 6. The Fishmarket was at that time the central section of the street now known as Buttermarket Street. Interestingly, a sixteenth-century map of Ipswich shows a row of three properties at the point indicated by the descriptors in the property transaction. Could this really represent the three units described in the transaction?

32 He was not the origin of the street name. It is more likely that it referred to cookshops.

33 Archdeaconry of Sudbury wills, IC 500/2/37/235.

34 KL/C 1623.

35 *Lynn Silver*, King's Lynn.

36 KL/C 1623.

37 *Lynn Silver*, King's Lynn.

38 KL/C48/2 1623.

39 NRO NCC 40 Beeles, 1555.

40 St Andrew's Parish Register 1558–1653, NRO PD 165/1.

41 LGC Minute Book KL ii.

42 Barrett, *Norwich Silver*, p. 82.

43 Millican, *Norwich Freemen*; Freemen Lynn.

44 *Lynn Silver*, King's Lynn, p. 17.

45 KL/ML2. An unnumbered MS in the King's Lynn Record Office.

46 Lincoln Consistory Court wills 1637/587.

47 Hawker, "Treasury", p. 11: "The Gosberton Chalice comes from a village near Boston, and is almost certainly the work of Edward Noddall, a goldsmith of Boston who died in 1636 or 1637. It is, therefore, the first piece of Boston work to have been identified"; see also Hawker, "Makers", p. 186.

48 Heal, p. 194.

49 L'Estrange and Rye, p. 123.

50 Adrian/Andrew is referred to in Katherine Baxter's (formerly Gilbert) will as occupying the former Gilbert workshop. (ESRO IC/AA1/33/126).

51 Barry and Brooks, p. 71.

52 Rye, p. 175.

53 *Norwich Mercury*, February 21–28, 1730.

Silver made in East Anglia, 1550–1750

Christopher Hartop

Is it possible to discern characteristics in style and decoration that are unique to silver made in East Anglia? Given the geographical separation of Norfolk and Suffolk, bounded on two-and-a-half sides by the sea, to the west by the Fens and heath and to the south by forest, as well as the local tradition, in Norfolk, to "do different", it would seem most likely in these counties at least. Can we see perhaps in their sixteenth-century church plate a continuation of the great artistic tradition of the later medieval period which produced distinct schools of illumination, painting and stained glass decoration?

The problem is that the evidence is patchy: survival for silver has always been haphazard. Until the establishment of the assay office in Norwich in 1565, it is not possible to identify with certainty any silver made there. Norfolk has thirty-eight surviving medieval patens, the greatest concentration of pre-Reformation patens in England. A few are struck with London hallmarks,[1] but it is likely that most of the rest were made locally. Spoons were the most common item of domestic silver; for example, the will of Thomas Brygge of Salle, dated 1444, lists twenty three[2] and by the end of the sixteenth century, to judge from the wealth of surviving examples, spoons were to be found in quite modest households like those of the yeoman farmers and city craftsmen, and were often given as christening presents (see nos. 65 and 66) or as memorials after death.[3]

More business has always meant the prospect of more irregularities in the trade. Therefore the periods which give us the best evidence in the form of datable silver are those of increased activity and corresponding regulation by means of marks. These are the 1560s, the prosperous 1620s and 1630s, and the late Stuart period. In Norfolk and Suffolk (which roughly constitute the extent of the Norwich diocese in the sixteenth century) there survive some four hundred pieces of Elizabethan church plate made in Norwich. There are also nearly a hundred ecclesiastical pieces from the same period made elsewhere in the region. Yet the surviving secular silver from this era numbers fewer than fifty pieces. For the seventeenth century, surviving objects number perhaps two hundred secular and slightly fewer church pieces. It is from the two main groups of survivors – Elizabethan communion cups and Stuart spoons – that one can make assessments of style and construction.

Before doing so, let us look at the position of the trade at the beginning of sixteenth century. A new problem had emerged for the provincial goldsmith – how to compete with his colleagues in London. Margaret Paston, writing in the mid fifteenth century from her townhouse in Norwich, had ordered her son to buy spoons during his visit to London. Whether she had done so because she felt London-made spoons were better quality, or cheaper, or that she felt London goldsmiths were more trustworthy than those in Norwich, is not known. The attraction of the exotic – luxury goods made in the capital – had always been there: the aristocracy and upper gentry had always had access to London shops; they were the "jet-set" who travelled back and forth between the court and their estates and were probably never major patrons of the local shops. How much of the 15,000 ounces of plate recorded at Caister Castle in 1458[4] had been made in Norfolk can only be guessed at. But with the rise of a new consumer base of lesser gentry and merchants in the Tudor period, the provincial goldsmiths had had to find ways of winning their custom. It was not merely a question of price, for the lion's share of the cost of any silver article was in the raw material, the price of which was consistent throughout the kingdom. It was a matter of liquidity that enabled the goldsmith not only to offer a large enough selection of goods for sale but also to withstand the often long intervals between delivery of and payment for goods. For this last reason, some goldsmiths appear to have kept "running cashes", an early form of banking which involved taking money on deposit, and for some, such as Simon Borrowe of Norwich, it is clear that this was their main way of earning a living.

The period of the Reformation had been one of feast or famine for the goldsmiths: vast quantities of plate from the monastic foundations had come on the market and had had to be converted to bullion. Parishes had taken the opportunity during the late 1540s to sell off much of their church plate and other valuables as it seemed likely they were about to be confiscated. In 1549 the Norwich goldsmith Felix Puttock had bought "crosses, chrysmatory, censeres, pix, chalice and ship" from St Andrew's church in Norwich for £79.[5] Contemporary accounts speak of "parlours hung with altar-cloths" and tables and beds covered with copes, and chalices used for beer.[6] After these losses there was a need to return to some form of dignity in the communion service; for instance, the churchwardens of Elmstead in Kent in 1560 complained that their vicar had:

> Yn the tyme of the popyshe masse he to reverence that order used to minister in a challyse of sylver; whereas now in contempte of this mynistracion he useth a bowle to unseemly to put mylke in.[7]

The chalice conversion programme initiated in England by Archbishop Parker in the 1560s provided a vast increase in business for the Norwich goldsmiths and led to the establishment of hallmarking there. It also saw the introduction of a new form of chalice, although the form of the cup does not seem to have been laid down in official documents. Why Parker was so keen not only to make sure that each parish had a "seemly cup" but to convert the existing chalices in every parish is not clear: there is no mention of communion cups in the writings of Zwingli and his followers. Moreover, no order for the conversion appears to have survived; one was submitted before Convocation in 1563 requiring that "chalices should be converted to decent cups" but it was rejected. When Parker, who was a Norwich man, visited the city in 1567, he was told by one of the prebendaries of the cathedral, George Gardiner, that "the communion is ministered in a chalice, contrary … to the Advertisements of the Queen",[8] but this must refer to some lost royal order, as Parker's Advertisements do not mention communion cups.

In his *Injunctions and Interrogaries*, issued in 1561, Bishop John Parkhurst of the Norwich diocese asked:

> Item, whether you do have in your church a decent pulpit and communion table furnished and placed as becometh, with a comely communion cup and a cover.[9]

Parkhurst had been one of the Marian exiles and was said by Cecil that he "winketh at schismatics and Anabaptists".

Fig. 7 Beaker, one of four originally belonging to the Dutch Church, Norwich, silver, Norwich, c.1575–80, maker's mark an orb and cross in shaped shield for William Cobbold (c.1530–1585/6) and a wyvern's head erased and incuse. *Norwich Castle Museum & Art Gallery*

Along with the bishops of Salisbury and Winchester he had given the congregation at Zurich a set of silver-gilt beakers for communion, so it is perhaps surprising that he did not encourage the adoption of the beaker rather than the cup for communion in East Anglia. The congregation of the Dutch Church in Norwich was to use beakers (fig. 7), as were other foreign congregations in Norfolk, but parish churches, perhaps because of some degree of conservatism, almost without exception purchased communion cups.

Thanks to their marks it is possible to establish a dated sequence of Norwich-made communion cups starting with 1565–6 and continuing until the date letter cycle seems to have been abandoned in 1571–2. Out of over four hundred pieces, more than three hundred and fifty have the date letter C for 1567–8, indicating the period of the most intense pressure on parishes to act. The size and quality of

Norwich-made cups, some with covers, vary enormously. Rich parishes could afford to pay the sometimes considerable sums needed to convert their chalices into cups large enough for their congregations, witness the churchwardens' accounts for St Mary Magdalen, Pulham, for 1567:

Ite payd for my dynner and horse meat when
    I caryed the chalys to Norwich   vj d
Ite payd at ye fetching home of ye communion
    cupe   iiij d
Ite payd for thre qrtrs and d I of sylver more
    that the Chalys did weye   iij s ix d
Ite payd for making of ye sayd cupe   vi s ij d[10]

Some churches, like All Saints, Knettisall, Suffolk (no. 70), were evidently unable to pay for the additional silver: their cup is a mere 4¾ inches high.

From the first marked examples, the form that was to become typical of the region is already apparent: a broad capacious bowl and spool-form stem often lacking a knop. In fact, evidence shows that this format was already established well before 1565–6: Thornage in north Norfolk has an unmarked cup of this form which can possibly be dated as early as 1563, for it is engraved THE FASHEN ALTRED B I STALON CLA 1563 (Stalon was the rector).[11]

Unlike the medieval chalice, whose form and proportions were strictly defined by doctrine, the protestant communion cup seems to have evolved out of a practical need. The early examples of the 1560s were clearly inspired by secular silver. It is tempting to see the London-made domestic goblet of 1531–2 from Wood Dalling (no. 5), which appears to have passed through the Cobbold shop in the 1560s, as inspiring the robust Norwich cups of the period, where the bowl dominates the stem.

Not only are Norwich-made cups often larger than those made in London, in many cases, especially with those from the Cobbold workshop, their quality and decoration are far superior. A good example is provided by the cup and cover from St Mary Coslany in Norwich (fig. 8). The bell-shaped bowl, also an unmistakably Norwich form, and the applied moulded bands, give the cup a horizontal emphasis that is uniquely East Anglian. On the far more modest cup from Swafield (fig. 9), the basic Norwich broad bowl sits on a spool-form stem without a knop, but the overall proportions are poor and the engraved band is clumsy compared to the distinctive border engraved between applied bands on the Coslany cup.

Fig. 8 Communion cup and cover of St Mary Coslany, Norwich, silver, parcel-gilt, Norwich, 1567–8, maker's mark an orb and cross in lozenge for William Cobbold (c.1530–1585/6). A well-proportioned and finely finished cup from one of the leading workshops of Elizabethan Norwich, its large size shows the wealth of this city parish. *Norwich Castle Museum & Art Gallery*

Engraving on silver was practised with great skill in the workshops of Germany and in particular the Low Countries, and it is probable that, as in London, the most skilled practitioners in Norwich were immigrants. The quality varies considerably, even among cups and other work bearing the same maker's mark. A comparison between the engraved bands on the St Mary Coslany cup and those on the one made in the same workshop for St Mary's, Diss (no. 3) shows the work of another hand and a different printed pattern source.

These bands of arabesques and mauresques had first

appeared in England in Thomas Geminus's book *Morysse and Damaskind Renewed and Encreased – Very Profitable for Goldsmyths and Embroyderers,* a book issued in London in 1548 which had been pirated from a book by Jacques Androuet de Cerceau. These motifs were ideal decoration for plain communion cups with an emphasis on line. A variation was the use of foliate scrolls of varying thickness, encountered on some work from the Cobbold shop like the Diss cup, but also on work by other makers such as the St Margaret's cup (fig. 3, p. 15) from Peterson's workshop, the tigerware jug, no. 6, and, most interestingly, on the ostrich egg cup, no. 93, and communion cups in the Colchester area from the Gilbert workshop. These bands copy the patterns of other designers

such as Bernard Solomon of Lyons. His pattern books, sold by the print shop of Jean de Tounes there in the 1550s, had a widespread circulation. It is likely that a skilled specialist engraver owning a copy of the book worked for more than one workshop in Norwich.

Bands of arabesques on East Anglian silver are often enclosed in strapwork cartouches formed of ruled borders containing zigzag, somewhat reminiscent of the continental form of assay gouge found on Norwich silver of the period (see p. 25). Zigzag bands are found on London silver, but they seem to have been most popular by far in East Anglia, especially on communion cups (see fig. 3, p. 15) and spoons (see Timothy Kent's essay, pp. 85–6).

The Cobbold workshop could also produce assured decorative lettering in the Lombardic alphabet, well-shown on the so-called Peterson cup, which probably dates from about 1580 (fig. 10), and the four communion beakers made for the Dutch Church in Norwich, which bear the Cobbold mark in conjunction with another unidentified mark of an incuse wyvern's head (fig. 7).[12] On these beakers, an attempt has been made to reproduce the engraved pendant foliate scrolls so popular on Dutch beakers of the period but it is done with far less fluency.

On Norwich silver, engraving is just one element which shows continental influence. The importance of the influx of foreign craftsmen into the city cannot be overestimated. They no doubt imported small silver items, such as dress hooks, from the Low Countries, as their London counterparts did, and may have retailed larger imported items such as the cup "of Flanders touch" mentioned in Peter Peterson's will. Hethel church has a superb domestic wine cup made in Ghent by Jan van Hauweghen in 1532. Communication with Amsterdam had always been as easy as with London, and the many busy ports along the coast (which nowadays survive as sleepy villages) conducted a vigorous trade not only with the Low Countries but also with Scandinavia and the Baltic. By the end of the fifteenth century Norwich already had an active community of immigrant merchants (the prosperous goldsmith Peter Peterson, "the Dutchman", admitted a freeman in 1553, appears to have been a third generation resident of Norwich). By 1572 there were perhaps 4,000 immigrants in Norwich, most of them weavers. The Dutch congregation rented the choir of the church of the Blackfriars on St Andrew's Plain and the Walloons used the Bishop's chapel. Like the Huguenot goldsmiths a century and more later in

Fig. 9 Communion cup of St Nicholas, Swafield, silver, Norwich 1566–7, maker's mark IV over a heart, for Valentine Isborne (fl. *c.*1556–after 1569) or possibly for John Vanderpoest (fl. before 1570–1606). A comparatively cheap example, inferior to the Coslany cup, for a small parish. *The Worshipful Company of Goldsmiths*

Fig. 10 The Peterson Cup, silver-gilt, Norwich, *c*.1575–86, maker's mark an orb and cross for William Cobbold (*c*.1530–1585/6). In 1574 Peter Peterson was excused from holding civic office except that of Chamberlain on payment of a "cup weying 15 ozs.". This cup, which weighs some 32 ounces, is engraved "THE MOST HERE IS DUNE BY PETER PETERSON" and was evidently refashioned by Peterson's colleague Cobbold with additional silver to make it match the size and decoration of two London-made cups in the civic collection. *The Corporation of Norwich*

London, the Dutch and Walloons no doubt provided a skilled workforce who were prepared to work harder and for less than their native counterparts.

Norwich in the late sixteenth century was a very cosmopolitan place, with perhaps as much as a quarter of the inhabitants speaking Dutch or French, and keeping their own identity into the seventeenth century. Well into the twentieth century Norfolk dialect retained Dutch words, and open spaces in Norwich are still called plains, from the Dutch *plein*. While in architecture the extent of the Dutch influence in the region has in recent years been revised (for instance, the gables of Raynham Hall were in fact inspired by Italy, not Amsterdam), in silver made in East Anglia it is still possible to identify some Netherlandish elements.

The assay gouge, mentioned above, is a distinctly continental feature on Norwich-made silver of this period (fig. 20, p. 36). In London and other assay centres in England, the silver was removed for testing by making a shallow, hardly visible, scrape. In towns in Germany and the Low Countries,

as well as in southern Europe, it was removed by gouging, leaving a pronounced zigzag line known in Germany as the *Tremulierstrich*.[13] With the exception of a few pieces marked in Edinburgh, it is found nowhere else in Britain. Its presence on pieces marked for 1565–6 onwards suggests that the first Norwich assayer (not necessarily the assay master) had trained on the continent.

It would be a mistake, however, to think of two distinct schools of silver existing in Norwich at this period, for the work bearing Peter Peterson's mark appears no more Dutch than objects from the Cobbold workshop. Both workshops doubtless employed immigrant journeymen, or used out-workers, and the continental elements are common to the work of both. Indeed, although Peterson died a much richer man than Cobbold (see pp. 39 and 43), the quality of his workshop's output was far inferior.

The late Charles Oman remarked on the high quality of the secular silver from the Cobbold workshop, singling out the Reade Salt (fig. 2, p. 14) as the most important piece of provincial silver of the period.[14] It is among the largest of Elizabethan drum salts, some fifteen inches high, and has chased decoration after Virgil Solis of foliage and fruit with strapwork panels at intervals. Yet the chasing, like that on the Peterson Cup (fig. 10), has a looseness and a lack of refinement that perhaps contradicts any suggestion that it may have been a London-made piece retailed by Cobbold. The armorial panels on the sides were originally enamelled, as was the shield held by the warrior on the cover, and there is no reason to doubt that such work was done in Norwich. It is more difficult to assess other components, however: the stamped egg and dart borders were produced with a cut-steel die that was expensive and difficult to make, and it tempting to think that sections of border, and cast components such as finials, were purchased from London workshops.

A look at the documentary evidence, although scant, perhaps sheds some light on this question. Of Cobbold's workshop, doubtless the largest in Norwich at the time, we have no records, and his will makes no mention of tools or stock, but there are surviving probate inventories of two of his contemporaries. That of Simon Borrowe,[15] of 1603, details a much smaller workshop than Cobbold's, and lists as stock only seven spoons, one beaker, five "pottes" each weighing just over three ounces, a "sylver taster wayinge iij oz." and quantities of thimbles, "claspes and eyes", "Jett ringes", "loose spearles, currale beades, and other trifles" with a total value of just over £35; the "toules together wt the sweepe of the shoppe" was priced at £10. It was clearly the sort of workshop where small silver items were made by raising and chasing and embellished by engraving, all activities done at a bench, but there is no evidence of the sort of large-scale drawing and casting that would be required to produce objects like the Reade Salt. John Gray's inventory, done in 1594,[16] lists more wrought plate, including a tankard, two salts weighing twenty ounces, "a tunn & a sylver Bowle weying 17 oz", "iij lipped potts" (i.e. mounted tigerware jugs such as no. 6), and five spoons as well as a quantity of rings and other jewellery, but the "working tooles & other implements" are only valued at 30s. As the debts outstanding to Gray were three times the value of his stock-in-trade, he seems to have been involved in banking more than making silver wares.

However, a different picture emerges from the will of Peter Peterson who, unlike Cobbold, seems to have had a workshop up to the time of his death and leaves his great-nephew "all my goldsmiths tools, stifles, hammers, ingotts, gouldsmithes bellows, and all my other saide tooles and patterns of leade belonging to my science". The presence of lead patterns is significant, for it shows that the type of work required to produce objects as elaborate as the Reade Salt was being carried out in Norwich. No doubt a good deal of interchange of patterns and casting took place between the major workshops: the finely finished dolphin scroll thumb-piece that embellishes the mount of the tigerware jug, no. 6, struck with a five-petalled rose, is also found on two flagons or bellied pots from Cobbold's workshop (fig. 11).

These pots are interesting conceits: their gilt straps are of a type normally used to mount ceramic bodies. Here they enclose white silver bodies. Two of similar form survive, both clearly for secular use although one has long been owned by Crostwight church. Struck with the Cobbold mark, their borders and cast components show the highest degree of finish. To produce them it required not only large-scale equipment to cast, solder, stamp and draw but also specialist technical and artistic skills of the highest order.

It is easy to understand how Norwich, the second city of the kingdom, could support one or more workshops on such a scale. The picture elsewhere in the region looks quite different, and it is evident that craftsmen competent in the techniques of raising and engraving moved according to demand, as frequently as Mary Fewster has observed (p. 18). They needed few items of expensive or cumbersome

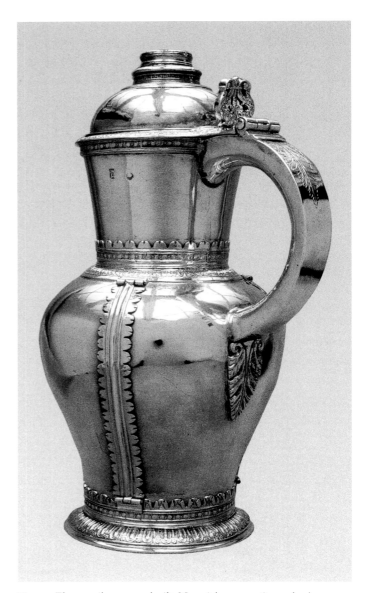

Fig. 11 Flagon, silver, parcel-gilt, Norwich, c.1575–80, maker's mark an orb and cross in shaped shield for William Cobbold (c.1530–1585/6). One of two jugs of this form from Cobbold's workshop, this example was formerly in the Rothermere Collection and acquired by Norwich Castle Museum in 1979. The other, of squatter form, belongs to All Saints Church, Crostwight, Norfolk, to whom it was given by a member of the Le Groos family some time after it became outmoded as a domestic object. *Norwich Castle Museum & Art Gallery*

equipment. Even large-scale soldering, which required a forge and skilful regulation of the temperature, could be avoided, as on the Bury St Edmunds cup, no. 91, where the stem is attached to the bowl by an overlapping hammered rim, not solder. The more intricate types of spoon finials, such as those of apostles, could be purchased ready made. For communion cups, the bowl could be raised and engraved at the bench. Only the distinctive Norfolk spool-form stem, often with moulded borders, was a more complicated affair and it could be that these were supplied by a specialist workshop.[17]

The surviving objects identified as locally-made from their marks from the period 1600 to 1660 shows how radically the business of silver production changed during this period. The investment in equipment and materials needed to run a workshop like Cobbold's, with so many specialists, could not be sustained once the church had been removed as a major customer and England descended into civil war. Demand was too spasmodic and the type of silver favoured by consumers was changing, too. Cups and tankards with strong outlines required little cast, die-struck or chased decoration. The

Fig. 12 (*right*) Cup and cover presented to Beeston St Lawrence by the Preston family in 1744, silver-gilt, Norwich, 1635–6, maker's mark of a pelican in her piety. *Norwich Castle Museum & Art Gallery*

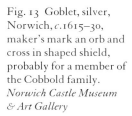

Fig. 13 Goblet, silver, Norwich, *c*.1615–30, maker's mark an orb and cross in shaped shield, probably for a member of the Cobbold family. *Norwich Castle Museum & Art Gallery*

simple goblet illustrated as fig. 13, with a mark that suggests it emanated from a workshop run by a descendant of William Cobbold, could be as late as the 1630s, although surviving London-marked examples with similar decoration date from as early as 1615. Its somewhat naïve rolled acanthus leaves chased on the bowl follow a standard form of the period but with little fluency. The sections of the baluster stem, which are each cast in two halves, are small enough to have been done in a comparatively modest workshop, yet the posssibility that ready-made stems of this form were purchased from suppliers in London should not be ruled out.

What commissions there were for communion cups during this period were often filled by cannibalizing what was left of the old cup, as with the cup from Swannington, no. 10, or with new secular goblets such as nos. 8 and 48. The first of these goblets is probably what is described as a wine cup in the following entry, while the second, larger, example with a broad bowl that would have been more suitable as a communion cup, is probably a "Beer cup":

May 3, 1634
Paid "… to Mr. Skottowe, Goldsmiths, for 3 Beer cups, wt. 44½ oz., and 3 wine cups, wt. 24½ oz., in all 68¾ oz. At 5/8 p. oz."[18]

Fig. 14 Communion cup and cover, part of the set made for Bishop Edward Reynolds (Bishop of Norwich, 1660–76), for use in his chapel, silver, Norwich, c.1665, maker's mark of Arthur Haslewood II (1638–84). *The Right Reverend the Bishop of Norwich*

Unfortunately Mr Skottowe's cups have not survived in the Norwich civic plate as they were remade by Arthur Haslewood II in about 1670.

The cup and cover belonging to Beeston church (fig. 12) is a secular piece made in Norwich in 1635–6.[19] Its intricate design incorporates anachronistic elements from twenty years before and its characterful if somewhat coarse chasing shows that the workshop that used a pelican as its mark could produce ambitiously decorated, albeit old-fashioned, work in the years leading up to the Civil War. Some seven years later, however, Timothy Skottowe was charged with directing quite a different sort of use for his workshop, to

… coin piss pots, bowls and flagons
Int' officers of horse and dragoons;
And into pikes and musqueteers
Stamp beakers, cups and porringers
Samuel Butler, *Hudibras* I, ii, pp. 565–8

The interruption in trade caused by the war was probably brief: by 1646 the quantity of silver assayed in London was already on the rise, and we can assume that the same recovery was under way in East Anglia. But when silver production did resume, the type of wares made in the region seems to have been confined to tankards, porringers and spoons, as well as the kind of small personal objects sold at fairs such as small beakers and dram or spirit cups. After the Restoration, improved communications meant that local goldsmiths could obtain ready-made components more easily, like the cast lion-form thumb-piece on the large-scale tankard, no. 20, but also that they faced stiffer competition from their colleagues in the capital. The Haslewood workshop (nos. 17–33) and an unidentified one (nos. 44–61) seem to have dominated silver production in the city in the 1660s and 70s; the finish and type of mouldings used on their respective products, however, suggest that there was little exchange of components between them as might have been the case a hundred years earlier. The distinctive bolection moulding found on the bases of beakers and tankards from the Haslewood workshop (nos. 20, 21 and 24) suggests their own work.

After its flowering in the sixteenth century, decorative engraving on East Anglian silver all but disappeared in the early Stuart period, as it did elsewhere. Engraving, however, did continue to be popular in the region for decorating spoon terminals (see pp. 85–6). After the Restoration, the ponderous crossed plumes popular in the 1660s can be found on work from Arthur Haslewood II, such as the Reynolds communion set (fig. 14), the tankard no. 20, and a saucepan in Norwich Castle Museum. These motifs were copied from contemporary heraldry manuals. There is nothing specifically local about this decoration, but an unmistakable feature of the Norwich silver of the 1670s and 80s is the superb calligraphic engraving found on a number of church pieces. Script with elaborate curlicues on the risers and descenders had some popularity on London-made silver in the 1660s, and a paten made for St Andrew's Church, Norwich, in the London workshop of the royal goldsmith Robert Smythier in 1665–6 has distinctive script that could be seen as the model used by the Norwich craftsman who went on to do such work for the Haslewood and Havers workshops. Good examples of this calligraphy include the Haslewood flagon at Stanhoe (fig. 15) and the Colkirk cup and cover (no. 30), while from the Havers

workshop we have the Bergh Apton cup and cover and a series of pieces made for the more prosperous Norwich churches in the 1670s. In contrast, objects in the "leopard's head and fleur-de-lis" group (nos. 44–61) are pricked rather than engraved. This could be taken to almost absurd lengths, as on the Paston flagon (no. 46) where the extensive inscription is done entirely by pricking. One exception is the attractive paten presented to Hardwick by Sir Peter Gleane in 1674 which has a circular inscription of decorative calligraphy which is similar to that found on the Haslewood/Havers examples, but done with a hesitancy and awkwardness that suggests an entirely different hand.

By the beginning of the eighteenth century there was still no doubt a closer relationship between an East Anglian goldsmith and his customer than there was in London. But the number of items which could be made in-house more cheaply than bought ready-made from suppliers in London was growing smaller and smaller, and the individuality that characterizes East Anglian silver of the sixteenth century was gone forever.

Fig. 15 Flagon of All Saints, Stanhoe, silver, Norwich, 1689–90, maker's mark of Elizabeth Haslewood (fl. 1684–1715). *The Worshipful Company of Goldsmiths*

1 Barrett, *Norwich Silver*, p. 14.
2 Cripps, p. 292.
3 The will of the Norwich goldsmith Peter Peterson's (see p. 43) lists numerous bequests of spoons inscribed "Remember Peterson".
4 Hartop, *Norwich Goldsmiths*, p. 5.
5 Barrett, *Norwich Silver*, p. 91.
6 Cripps, p. 218.
7 *Archaeologica Cantiana*, 1886, vol. 16, p. 337.
8 Strype, *Life of Archbishop Parker*, London 1821, vol. 3, p. 159.
9 Second Report of the Ritual Commissioners 1868, Appendix E, p. 105.
10 NRO/Parish Records/Pulham St Mary.
11 NA Holt, p. 50.
12 The beakers were sold "by order of the Trustees of the Church", Christie's, London, June 18, 1891, lot 150; one is in Norwich Castle Museum & Art Gallery, another in the Rijksmuseum, Amsterdam, and two in the Ashmolean Museum, Oxford.
13 See I. Dombi, B. Höfler & I. Loschek: *Bruckmann's Silber-Lexicon*, Munich, 1982, p. 296. The encyclopedia *Grosse Brockhaus*, Wiesbaden, 1957, however, uses the word *Tremolierstich*.
14 Oman, "Civic Plate", p. 229.
15 NRO NCC INV/19 152B 1603; Hartop, *Norwich Goldsmiths*, pp. 43–4; for a discussion of "claspes and eyes" see D. Gaimster, M. Hayward, D. Mitchell & K. Parker: "Tudor silver-gilt dress-hooks: a new class of treasure find in England" in *Antiquaries Journal*, 2002, vol. 82, pp. 157–96, and D. Thornton & D. Mitchell: "Three Tudor dress-hook" in ibid., 2003, vol. 83, pp. 486–91.
16 Levine, "Norwich Goldsmiths' Wills", p. 485.
17 I am grateful to Mary Fewster and Nigel Bumphrey for this idea.
18 NRO Norwich Court Book.
19 The cup was not known to have a cover until recently when one was identified as such by Nigel Bumphrey.

Norwich

A few years ago, archaeologists excavating the site of the proposed Millennium Library in Norwich discovered a Viking gold ingot, crucible fragments with traces of gold, and lead oxide, showing that working in precious metal is as old as the city itself.[1] Norwich had its own mint and from the reign of Athelstan and until the time of Henry III coins were minted there continuously.[2] "Solomon the Goldsmith" features in records in 1141, and throughout the fourteenth and fifteenth centuries Norwich appears to have supported a thriving community of goldsmiths.

In 1423 Norwich was one of several towns in England appointed to have a "touch" and assay gold and silver as the London company of goldsmiths did, but it seems the Norwich guild never exercised this right, for in 1565 they petitioned the Mayor to do so, stating that "no ... towche or Standerde have been hitherto appoynted or assynged unto the said artificers".[3] The date of 1565 is significant. Archbishop Parker was directing dioceses to convert the old massing chalice into a "seemly communion cup". Whether the Norwich goldsmiths anticipated this dramatic increase in business and sought to get their own house in order, or whether they were prompted to do so by the London company is not known.

The first Norwich hallmarks appear with the date letter A for 1565–6; the cycle was abandoned with the G for 1571–2 but the town mark, the civic arms of a castle and lion, continued to be used into the seventeenth century. An incuse G appears on two James I cups and may be evidence of another date letter cycle (see p. 45). In 1611 in the mayor's court "a proclamacion from the Counsell was delivered concerning goldsmythes" but nothing further appears to have been done until 1622 when the Norwich guilds were reorganized and the appointment of assay masters was again recorded. In 1624 new laws governing the goldsmiths were enacted[4] which reiterated that "the Touch for the said Company of Goldsmythes wthin this City or liberties thereof shalbe the Stamps wth the Castell & Lyon under". In addition to the town mark and date letter, a new mark of a crowned rose, which seems to have been used as a standard mark, appears.[5]

From about the same time is an undated "Oath of the Strangers Goldsmiths" in the civic records, reflecting the continuing influxes from the fifteenth century onwards of foreign workman, mostly from the Low Countries.[6]

The new date letter cycle continued until the T of 1642–3 when it was abandoned with the growing hostilities of the Civil War. Rose, crown and Norwich town marks in various forms appear again after about 1645 but whether these were official stamps of the guild or were goldsmiths' own versions of the previous official marks is unclear. The same punches seem to have been used on silver from the Haslewood workshop and that bearing the mark of William Haydon, but insufficient examples from this period exist to enable a systematic study to be made. A further, completely different, set of marks that may best be called the "leopard's head and fleur-de-lis" group are clearly in imitation of hallmarks. These marks were used by an unidentified workshop in Norwich up to the 1680s (nos. 44–61).

With the Restoration, the castle and lion punches and now separate ones of the rose and crown were of a higher quality and greater consistency than before, suggesting that the processes of assaying and marking were again on an official level, at least to a limited extent. There are exceptions such as the "leopard's head and fleur-de-lis" group. A beaker and a spoon are recorded struck with the mark of Robert Osborne (free in 1665) and with his own version of the castle and lion and the crown. However, the "official" version of the marks is the most common, found in conjunction with the marks of at least six different makers until 1688 when, with the Glorious Revolution, a new date letter cycle was started. The Haslewood, Havers and Daniell shops seem to have been the largest in the city, but other maker's marks do appear. The date letter cycle breaks down with the D of 1691–2 and resumes with the I of 1696–7[7] but in 1697, with the Britannia Silver Act, assaying and marking outside London were discontinued. The Norwich goldsmiths, finding themselves without the means to mark their wares locally, and faced with the prospect of having to send everything to London to be assayed, petitioned Parliament the following year. But it was not until 1701 that a new bill permitting assaying and marking to start again in several provincial cities, including Norwich, was passed. In the interim some makers devised their own versions of the new Britannia marks (nos. 39 and 40) or struck their silver with just their maker's mark (nos. 32 and 33).

Only a handful of pieces survive struck with the new Norwich Britannia hallmarks (fig. 5, p. 17). While it is clear that some silver continued to be made in the city in the early years of the eighteenth century,[8] the shops found it increasingly difficult to compete with the large-scale work-shops in London and sold fewer of their own products, although they still could melt scrap.

The *Norwich Mercury* of July 31, 1736 reported:

> Norwich, Last Wednesday one Samuel Yemms went to Mr. Harwood's shop in the Market-place, and offered to sell a Piece of Plate, which appeared to be some Plate cut in pieces, and very much Battered; upon which he was stopt and searched, and several other pieces were found in his Pockets; and being carried before Mr Mayor, he there confess'd it was stolen out of a House at Wisbech, and his wife is in Wisbech Gaol on Account of the said Robbery. The said Yemms is committed to our Gaol.

The Harwood and Haslewood shops carried on well into the eighteenth century, whereas the shop of the Roes (father and son) spans almost the whole of that century. In the 1730s, Nathaniel Roe I was commissioned by the city to supply silver for the Lord Mayor's table. What survives of this group was made in London by leading specialist manufacturers. Nathaniel Roe II, who was the last goldsmith to be admitted a freeman of Norwich, put on a show of James Cox automata in his shop in the 1770s. By then shops like these were retailing jewellery, plate and "toys" (small luxury goods such as snuffboxes, *étuis*, buttons etc.) and probably only main-taining small workshops for repairs, alterations, engraving and the manufacture of some small items. This was a new role for the provincial goldsmith, one that was to continue in English towns and cities well into the twentieth century.

1 Ayres, pp. 32–3.
2 Hudson and Tingey, p. cxliii.
3 The petition is printed in full in Jackson, pp. 327–30.
4 See Pierce Gould where the document is printed in full.
5 Besides being the town mark of Dordrecht, the crowned rose was also used in other parts of England in the first half of the seventeenth century. Seal-top and apostle spoons exist struck with a crowned rose either singly in the bowl or in both the bowl and on the back of the stem. Such spoons, where the crown, unlike the Norwich mark, is open, were included in the *Ellis Catalogue*, lots 45–8 and attributed by Commander How to Norwich, but later, in an article in *Apollo* (How, "Criticisms", p. 152), he suggested a West Country,

possibly Taunton, origin for them on account of the casting of their terminals. This is a view endorsed more recently by Timothy Kent. The punches used for these crowned rose marks are larger than those used in Norwich.
6 Printed in Hudson and Tingey, p. 313, no. CCCCXXI.
7 It may well be that the date letter D continued to be used until 1696. The quantity of objects that have survived with the D, and the fact that some have dates inscribed on them after 1691–2 (such as the basin dated 1694, no. 42) suggest that this was the case. Cut steel punches of high quality were costly and it easy to understand why the assay master may have been loath to incur the expense of changing them unless prompted by the London company. Interestingly the beaker (no. 24) bearing the date letter for 1696–7 shows a crack across the die suggesting that mark was struck at the end of the die's life.
8 The London company searchers visited Norwich and fined goldsmiths for offering substandard wares in 1703, 1705, 1706, 1707 as well as in 1719.

The guildhall of the Norwich company of goldsmiths

Christopher Garibaldi

Traditionally it has been held that the Norwich goldsmiths' hall and assay office had long ago been demolished and that no pictorial records survive to show us what the buildings might have looked like. Indeed, previous publica-tions have perpetuated this notion,[1] even asserting that any remains there might be lay hidden beneath the present-day Jarrold's department store.[2]

However, it can now be shown that not only was the Norwich goldsmiths' hall not at this site but that it is in fact depicted prominently (albeit slightly disguised) in a number of views of the Norwich market-place.[3] And most excitingly of all, the buildings have in fact survived in a remarkably complete form to this day with part of the vaults and cellars currently home to a wine bar.

Francis Blomefield's eighteenth-century *History of the County of Norfolk*[4] is the main source for positioning the hall, but his information has been consistently misinter-preted. The fourth volume of this ambitious, extremely detailed and in the main highly reliable survey of the county and of Norwich contains the following description:

> The north end of the *market-place* from *Dove-lane*[5] to *Smethe-rowe*[6] aforesaid, was the *Aurifabria,* or *Goldsmiths-rowe;* and the lane aforesaid was called *Smethy-lane,* from the working *goldsmiths* that lived there: the messuage called the *Stone-hall,* in 1286 belonged to John le Brun, founder of the chapel in the Fields, was his dwelling-house, and afterwards was made (73) The GOLDSMITHS-HALL; and it seems as

if they rebuilt it, for there remain many ancient shields of arms in the stone-work to this day.

The number 73 refers to a map bound in with the volumes (fig. 16). Only when this map is assumed to be to scale does the site of the hall come within the area now occupied by Jarrold's.[7] If, on the other hand, it is supposed that Blomefield map was not to scale a rather different picture emerges with the hall much farther to the west, on the north side of the market-place in the area just below the Guildhall. This area, now called Guildhall Hill is within the area known as early as 1286 as "Vicus de Aurifabria" and from 1372 as "Le Goldsmytherowe".[8] Blomefield states that the goldsmiths' hall was built on the site of a building known as "Stone-Hall" which in 1286 had belonged to a John le Brun.[9] The Norwich Survey which maps the Norwich Enrolled Deeds of 1285 to 1341 confirms the existence of a deed of 1287 referring to the property of Sir John le Brun called "Stonhalla" and establishes that it was situated behind the north side of the market, in a small courtyard behind the Guildhall Hill row of shops, just to the east of Dove Street (at that time called "Holtor").[10]

Blomefield also refers to the "many ancient shields of arms in the stone-work" of the hall. If we look at a view of the north side of Norwich market-place painted by Robert

Dighton in 1799 (fig. 17) we can see in the background, slightly to the right of centre, a handsome four-storey brick façade of the late seventeenth or early eighteenth century.[11] It has nine bays or windows on the first and second floors above four shop fronts on the ground floor and is enlivened with quoins. On the right hand side of the slightly projecting central three-bayed section a set of stone emblems can be clearly seen arranged one above the other. These stone devices represent variously a coat of arms comprising a shield placed diagonally above something that might well be a goldsmith's stake and below this an anvil-like object. The presence of the latter would be entirely consistent with the fact that the Sixth Grand Company created by the 1622 reforms amalgamated many of the Norwich craft guilds among them saddlers, ironmongers and blacksmiths as well as goldsmiths. On the ground floor, in the centre of the row of shops is an open passageway through which a courtyard and a further building may be glimpsed. It is this inner building which occupies the site of John le Brun's medieval Stone-Hall.

What we therefore have before us is the building Blomefield designated "Goldsmiths' Hall". The arrangement of the shop fronts in Dighton's painting can also be clearly seen in David Hodgson's sketch of Guildhall Hill

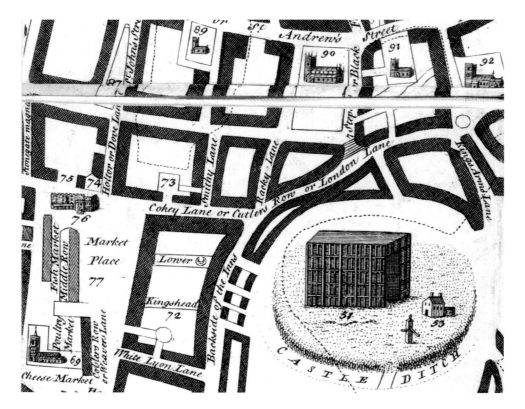

Fig. 16 Detail of the map of the city of Norwich from Francis Blomefield's *Essay towards a Topographical History of the County of Norfolk, c.1760.* Goldsmiths' Row ran along the north-east side of the Market Place and the author here suggests that the gold-smith's guild hall, marked as 73, was in fact a short distance to the west on the Market Place itself. *Norwich Castle Museum & Art Gallery*

Fig. 17 *Norwich Market Place* by Robert Dighton, 1799, showing in the centre what may have been the goldsmiths' guildhall. The building still houses shops at street level and the one farthest to the right was, until the 1930s, a silversmith's. *Norwich Castle Museum & Art Gallery*

from 1827 and in one of the earliest photographs of Norwich taken in the mid 1850s (possibly by G. M. Mason) (fig. 18). The presence of the coats of arms and emblems on the outside of the building suggests a proprietary link between the shops and the courtyard building. Such an arrangement was in all likelihood to provide a central and highly visible presence for one of the most important of Norwich's trade guilds whilst ensuring a mechanism for raising significant income from the shops in one of the most commercially important areas of the city. There are parallels in the practice of a number of livery companies in the City of London whose halls both ancient and modern have adopted a similar strategy to maximize income generation on a prestigious city centre site.[12]

In the centre of the front row of shops facing the market-place is a striking feature in Dighton's 1799 view, in subsequent photographs, and still visible to this day. On the first floor the central window, unlike any of the others, has a stone frame and a large pediment. Although further detailed structural investigation needs to take place on site, it is possible that this external architectural feature reflected an

Fig. 18 (*right*) Photograph of Guildhall Hill, *c.*1855, showing clearly the archway leading to the inner courtyard with a curious pedimented window above. *Norwich County Council Library & Information Service*

internal division of space whereby a small viewing room was accessed separately from the shop premises on either side. Even if this were not the case and the central window turns out to have been simply an external architectural conceit, it was certainly a significant position from which senior officers of the company such as wardens could view and perhaps more importantly be seen during ceremonies and other civic events. Somewhat later, it may have been from this vantage point that John Sell Cotman painted his famous water-colour, *Norwich Market Place* (*c*.1809).[13] Cotman had made an earlier sketch from a window over the shop of the silver-smith Mr Cooper, in the north-east corner of the market-place,[14] but the later work was painted in a more central position on the north side of the square. In addition, the prominent position of the goldsmiths' hall complex can be appreciated from a number of early photographs of great events taking place on Guildhall Hill such as the proclama-tion of Edward VII in 1901 or the Armistice in 1918. The central function of this portion of the market square was lost with the building of the new City Hall between 1932 and 1938 when a number of buildings adjacent to the Guildhall were also demolished.

Until when was the goldsmiths' hall used by the guild? Was 1622 a turning point? It is interesting to note that the Ordinances for Crafts of that year had placed the newly formed Sixth Grand Company under the control of the

alderman of the ward of East Wymer, which excluded Guildhall Hill.[15] Furthermore, the statutes governing the craft of the goldsmiths enacted by the Norwich Assembly in 1624 specifically charge that they should meet "at the Newhall" within the city which was the name by which St Andrew's Hall was commonly known.[16] The statutes also allow for "some other convenient place by them to be appointed" but it seems strange that if a prominent building in the centre of the city was already owned by the company that the highly specific statutes should fail to mention it. Later on the city's goldsmiths are instructed to bring all their silver to the wardens for assay and are even given the times and days when this is possible but there is no mention of a specific goldsmiths' hall.

Several other interesting questions remain. If the company did in fact own both hall and shops, how long had this arrangement been in place? Since when did the Company own the whole of this prestigious site and when exactly was each of the buildings constructed? Was this major building project perhaps one of the reasons why senior goldsmiths in Norwich failed to continue as makers (rather than simply retailers) beyond the first years of the eighteenth century, thus making the need for an assay office redundant? How long did the goldsmiths' hall and indeed the company con-tinue to function after the lapse of the assay office and until when did the building continue to be commonly known as the goldsmiths' hall?

Some of the answers to these fascinating questions may still emerge from a comprehensive survey of the extant architecture or from systematic archival research on each of the buildings concerned but at least we now know that we are looking in the right place.

During the research for this article, an interesting set of water-colour and pencil drawings came to light in the Norwich Castle collections.[17] Dated 1851, they were drawn by Cornelius Janson Walter Winter (?1817–1891) and carry the title *Embossed bricks from a house in London Street, Norwich*. (fig. 19). One of the bricks is embossed with the coat of arms of the goldsmiths' company. Together with the survival of the Basyngham Gateway (fig. 22) which also bore the goldsmiths' arms, the bricks would suggest that it was not unusual for the goldsmiths of Norwich to adorn their premises with, in addition to any personal arms to which they may have been entitled, those of their trade.

Fig. 19 Embossed bricks from a house in London Street by C. J. Winter, 1851. The arms of the goldsmiths' company appear lower right. *Norwich Castle Museum & Art Gallery*

1 Barrett, *Norwich Silver*, p. 11.

2 Emmerson, p. 5.

3 See also Jonathan Mardle [Eric Fowler], "A fine Norwich Building" in the *Eastern Daily Press*, June 20, 1973.

4 Blomefield has remained the definitive source book for Norwich.

5   Now Dove Street.

6   Now Little London Street.

7   Barrett, *Norwich Silver*, p. 11.

8   Ibid., p. 11.

9   In many cases Blomefield relied on and expanded the work in manuscript of John Kirkpatrick's *Streets and Lanes of the City of Norwich* (written before 1728 but not published until 1889). However, in this case although Kirkpatrick describes Goldsmiths-rowe he does not mention either the goldsmiths' hall or John le Brun.

10 City Court Rolls (Enrolled Deeds and Wills), Norfolk Record Office/NCR Case 1; The Norwich Survey, NRO/MC146 includes indexes to enrolled deeds and 137 maps showing property ownership from 1285 to 1341 based on information from the rolls.

11 Pevsner asks "Is it all of *c.*1700?", Pevsner, p. 273.

12 The recently completed new hall of the Worshipful Company of Haberdashers in London adopts a similar pattern.

13 Tate Collection (No5636).

14 Moore, pp. 13–19.

15 The site of the goldsmiths' hall on Guildhall Hill fell within the ward of Mancroft.

16 St Andrew's Hall also fell outside the ward of East Wymer, being in Mid Wymer.

17 1951.235.B532/3/4.

Possible attributions for four maker's marks from sixteenth-century Norwich

Colin Ticktum

As is well known, there was no official system for the marking of plate in Norwich until the establishment of the assay office there in 1565. To date nine makers' marks have been recorded in conjunction with Norwich hallmarks for the following four years, of which five have been attributed.[1] Those so far unidentified are: a trefoil, the so-called maiden-head, an estoille and a Tudor rose. The purpose of this article is to put forward possible attributions for these marks. The first three marks appear on a considerable number of objects and must have been the marks of important makers. The Tudor rose mark is found on only a handful of pieces, all from 1568–9, but I have made a suggestion. The trefoil is the one mark that could possibly date from before 1565.

This investigation began in 1997 when we acquired a slip-end spoon (no. 1) in a box of items at a local auction. The auctioneers said that it had come from a local estate where it had been for generations. I was very surprised to find an identical example illustrated in How's *English Silver Spoons*,[2] one of a set of three puzzlingly described as Continental. My example clearly was not the one in the illustration, although the mark and the basic form were the same. All the spoons in this group are, I believe, English and date from the sixteenth century.[3]

One of the problems with objects which may have originated in Norwich prior to 1565 is that we do not know what, if any, marks would have been stamped on them. The date letter cycle started in 1565 seems to have lasted only until 1571–2 (letters A to G), and objects from that six-year period should have a town mark, date letter and maker's mark. Having discussed our spoon at length with the late Geoffrey Barrett, the conclusion reached is that it probably dates from the 1550s. This suggests that this spoon, and the other similar examples listed by How, could be the only Norwich pieces bearing a maker's punch to have survived from before the opening of the assay office. Is it possible to associate this trefoil mark to a named Norwich goldsmith?

Candidate for the trefoil mark: William Rogers

William Rogers was born at Lyng in the 1520s. His father was named John and he had an uncle, also William, who was a grocer and in 1543 mayor of Norwich.[4] It may be that the uncle was instrumental in apprenticing William in London to Jasper Palmer, a spoon maker; he obtained his freedom around 1550 by purchase.[5] In 1557, the year his uncle died, William returned to Norwich and set himself up in business, very possibly having received a legacy which enabled him to do so. There is therefore a period of eight years, 1557–65, when William Rogers would have been making silver in Norwich without the ability to mark his work fully.

In 1569 a search was made by the London goldsmiths' company of Stourbridge Fair, Cambridge, where William Rogers was plying his trade.[6] Three of his spoons were found to be sub-standard and broken, all of them slip-ends. His apprentice, Christopher Tanner, made slip-end spoons – a skill he must have acquired from his master. That Rogers made spoons is indisputable. Interestingly, Charles Oman in his *English Church Plate*, when discussing the cup belonging to St Lawrence, Norwich, which has the maker's mark of a trefoil, comments: "the form of the finial on the cover should specially be noted. It was probably cast from the model for a spoon knob …"[7]

William Rogers was joint warden with William Cobbold when the assay office opened, the following year with Peter Peterson I, and the year after, 1567, with Cobbold again. These are the three most important names in the Norwich guild at the time of the opening of the assay office.

Only two pieces of silver have so far come to light from the first year of assay, 1565–6, both by Cobbold. From the following year, 1566–7, thirteen pieces are known, five of which bear the trefoil mark. Subsequent years also see a large number of objects with the trefoil mark. The London goldsmiths' company records show that Rogers was still working in Norwich in 1575.[8]

Having seen many slip-end spoons, I believe that the spoon under discussion dates to the late 1550s. The position of the mark is at the base of the stem (a placing usually associated with London-made spoons) rather than in the bowl, as one might expect on a provincial piece. William Rogers may well have established his mark as the trefoil before he returned to Norwich, and continued to use it there. Not having other marks available to him prior to the establishment of the local assay office, it would have been consistent for him to position his mark as he would have done when in London. I have found only one instance of a trefoil mark being used by a London maker—in the fifteenth century.[9] The slip-end spoon under discussion does not appear to be that early and, if it had been made in London in the sixteenth century, it would have been struck with other London marks.

It would seem that William Rogers could not have been the owner of the two other marks that have survived on numerous objects. The estoille mark does not appear until 1567–8 (and Rogers must have been operating before then). The "maidenhead" mark ceases in 1568 (and Rogers continued beyond that date). The trefoil mark is recorded before and after the "maidenhead" mark.

Candidate for the estoille mark: George Fenne

The estoille mark is, in my view, probably the easiest of the three marks to attribute on the basis of current information. I believe it to be the mark of George Fenne. His father was Dutch, born in Utrecht, and George Fenne became an important citizen of Norwich. In 1587 he became "leading elder" of the Dutch congregation and he was warden of the

guild in 1570, 1576 and 1587. One of his apprentices was Matthew Cobbold, son of William, who became free in 1593. George Fenne died in his forties, in 1592.[10]

The first appearance of the estoille mark is in 1567–8, which coincides exactly with his freedom, by purchase, in 1567. The dates seem to be too much of a coincidence not to be connected.

Candidate for the "maidenhead" or "queen's head" mark: John Basyngham

The attribution of this mark is more speculative. Having ascribed the trefoil and the estoille marks to two of the most prominent citizens and goldsmiths of the day, there are no other major names at the time of the opening of the assay office that enter into the reckoning.

Before discussing a possible attribution, the mark itself should be identified. It is not clear who coined the description "maidenhead". The depiction is certainly that of a woman's head, but the woman looks to me to be Queen Elizabeth, in a Tudor headdress and with no religious connotation. The description "queen's head" therefore seems more suitable for this mark.

Certain criteria need to be met in ascribing the mark. The maker has to be free and working around the time of the opening of the assay office, as the mark is first seen in 1566–7. A good training from one of the other major makers is suggested, since the articles on which the mark appears are primarily church pieces of good quality. Thirdly, a degree of experience would have been required to make such pieces. The list of possible candidates whom I have so far identified is as follows:

> *Phylyppe Carver*, in 1545 he made a new chape and double H crowned for the civic sword
> *John Basyngham I*, free 1517; very wealthy goldsmith; died in 1569
> *John Basyngham II*, free 1539; alive in 1555 and working; he had as an apprentice Peter Peterson I
> *William Umfrey*, free 1547; free by patrimony; nothing else known of him
> *Thomas Warlowe*, free 1549; apprenticed to Felix Puttock; recorded as poor in the survey of 1570, when he was aged about 60
> *Zachary Shulte*, free 1548; an immigrant allowed to practise; nothing known
> *Zacharias Shulte*, free 1560; son of Zachary; nothing known
> *Richard Waterman*, free 1560; apprenticed to William Cobbold; moved to King's Lynn in 1567
> *Walter Mann*, free 1562; apprenticed to William Cobbold; nothing else known[11]

Fig. 20 (*above left*) Norwich hallmarks for 1567–8 and maker's mark a trefoil slipped, from the cup of All Saints, Swanton Morley (cat. no. 2)

Fig. 21 (*above right*) Norwich hallmarks for 1566–7 and maker's mark a maidenhead, from the cup of St Andrew, Letheringsett

Fig. 22 *The Basyngham Gateway*, etching by H. E. Blazeby, *c.*1850. Originally the gateway to a house in London Street built by John Basyngham I, the prominent goldsmith, it is embellished with the arms of Henry VIII, the city of Norwich and the goldsmiths' company. Extensively restored, it was moved to its present position in the south front of the Guildhall in 1857 when a portion of London Street was demolished. *Norwich Castle Museum & Art Gallery*

Fig. 23 Communion cup of St Peter, Matlaske, silver, Norwich, 1567–8, maker's mark an estoille. *The Worshipful Company of Goldsmiths*

Some of these names can be eliminated as they do not appear to meet the basic criteria. Phylyppe Carver was probably at least 60 years old when the assay office opened. The two Shultes and William Umfrey are also very unlikely candidates: the former were not local and it is unlikely they could have gained the prominence necessary to produce quality work; nothing is known of the latter. Thomas Warlowe, although apprenticed to Felix Puttock, seems to have been in dire financial straits in later life and I find it hard to believe that someone who made the amount of silver recorded with this mark during 1565–70 could have been as poor as he was; the only articles associated with him were coat hooks.[12]

Four possible candidates are left: John Basyngham I and II, Richard Waterman and Walter Mann. Details of the last two are limited: both had the right background, being apprenticed to William Cobbold, and they were free well before 1565. They therefore had the right connections to get some of the orders that overwhelmed the trade, especially in 1567–8. But Richard Waterman appears to have left Norwich for King's Lynn before the date (1568–9) when the maidenhead mark is known to have last been used; and little or nothing is known of Walter Mann.

Weight of evidence seems to point to the Basynghams. The dates of their respective freedoms makes them candidates, though whether they are father and son or uncle and nephew and whether the workshop was a family business are still unknown. They appear to have had the skill, experience and contacts to produce the significant amounts of silver involved.[13] The maidenhead or queen's head mark does not seem to have been used after 1568–9; John Basyngham I died in 1569. John II is referred to in his will and would probably have been in his late fifties at the time. If the mark was that of a workshop rather than an individual, John II may well have decided to close it and retire if he inherited a significant legacy on the death of John I.

The Basynghams were apparently staunch protestants and also supporters of the Elizabethan settlement. The gateway preserved at the south-west corner of Norwich Guildhall was originally the entrance to John I's house in Cutler Row. It incorporates the royal arms together with those of the city and the goldsmiths' company. A family with such loyalties might well have chosen a representation of the young queen as their mark, especially as the opening of the assay office in 1565 came only seven years after her accession. The attribution of a mark that could be described as that of a queen's head to a Basyngham workshop seems highly probable on the basis of current information.

Candidate for the Tudor rose mark?

An added thought, but a matter of conjecture, is that the Tudor rose mark, another symbol of Queen Elizabeth, which appears only in 1568–9, might be ascribed to John Basyngham II, if indeed he carried on the workshop after John I's death. The situation might be clarified if a date of death for John II could be found.

1 They are: William Cobbold (orb and cross), Peter Peterson I (sun in splendour), Thomas Buttell (flat fish), Valentine Isbourne (IV over heart), and Christopher Tanner (CT).
2 Vol. 2, p. 308 and plate 12.
3 Comparing these spoons with those described as English in the earlier chapters of How, *Spoons*, vol. 1, such as p. 84, plate 4 (from the Benson Collection) and p. 278, plate 1, section x (from the Dor Collection), I cannot see any significant difference between these and the slip-end spoons under discussion.
4 Information from Mary Fewster.
5 Information from Mary Fewster.
6 Barrett, *Norwich Silver*, p. 91.
7 Oman, *Church Plate*, p. 196.
8 Barrett, *Norwich Silver*, p. 92; information from Mary Fewster.
9 Jackson, p. 340.
10 Barrett, *Norwich Silver*, p. 84; information from Mary Fewster.
11 Ibid., p. 89.
12 Information from Mary Fewster.
13 Barrett, *Norwich Silver*, passim, and also information from Mary Fewster.

1

1

Slip-end spoon *Silver*

? Norwich; ? *c.* 1557–1565; maker's mark a trefoil in outline punch

The Ticktum Collection

With fig-shaped bowl and hexagonal flared stem

For a discussion of this spoon and a possible attribution of its mark to of William Rogers (fl. 1550–after 1575) see pp. 35–6.

L. 6⅛ in. (15.5 cm)

Mark: struck on back of stem with a trefoil in an outline punch

2

Communion cup *Silver*

Norwich; 1567–8; maker's mark a trefoil in shield-shaped punch

All Saints Church, Swanton Morley, Norfolk

On domed foot with an egg-and-dart border, rising to a spool-form stem (without knop) and tapering straight-sided bowl engraved between two zigzag bands: SWANTON MORLAY AL SAYNTES AÑO 1567

For a discussion of this mark and its possible attribution to William Rogers (fl. 1550–after 1575), see pp. 35–6.

H. 7⅛ in. (18 cm); DIAM. 4½ in. (10.7 cm); WEIGHT 10 OZ. (311 g)

Marks: Struck on rim with castle and lion and date letter upper-case roman C in square punch (Jackson, p. 336, line 3) and with maker's mark (Levine, no. 11)

Published: NA Elmham, *sub* Swanton Morley

2

William Cobbold was apprenticed to Thomas Bere and admitted a freeman in 1552.[3] He lived in Cutler Row, now London Street, between St Andrew's and Swan Lane in the parish of St Andrew.[4] The registers of the church of St Andrew, for which he was churchwarden in 1581, record the baptisms of his children but there is no mention of his burial.[5] Cobbold's will, witnessed by Peter Peterson, goldsmith (see p. 43), George Birch, apothecary, and Richard Lussher, scrivener, was signed on May 13, 1585 and proved on March 18, 1585/6. His legacies totalled £111 14s 10d showing him to have been prosperous but not as wealthy as his colleague, Peter Peterson.[6] One son, William, evidently the eldest, was left all his real property after the death of Cobbold's widow. Another son followed him into the goldsmiths' trade: Matthew Cobbold was left £13 5s 8d.[7] He had been apprenticed to the goldsmith George Fenne in 1583 and was admitted free in 1593 and buried in St Andrew April 22, 1604.[8]

1 Levine, p. 294.
2 NA, Norwich, p. 88.
3 Freemen, Norwich, p. 70.
4 NRO, Langable Rents, 1570.
5 In his will he is described as "late of the cittie of Norwich" and, as there is no mention of stock or tools, it is likely he had retired outside the city (NRO/Nch. Arch. Ct. Wills 1584 O.W. 80); see Levine, "Norwich Goldsmiths' Wills", p. 484.
6 Levine, p. 295.
7 Hartop, *Norwich Goldsmiths*, p. 39.
8 Levine, p. 295.

William Cobbold (c.1530–1585/6)

(Cat. nos. 3 and 4)

William Cobbold was not the most prosperous of the Elizabethan goldsmiths of Norwich, but work bearing his mark is the finest to survive. The mark attributed to him is an orb and cross which appears in variously shaped punches. The mark was linked to Cobbold by the late George Levine through an entry in the churchwardens' accounts for St John Maddermarket, Norwich, for 1567: "pd. Cobbold making and gylding ye communion kup with 3 qts. Silver 39s 7d".[1] The cup is struck with an orb and cross in a lozenge.[2] Levine suggested that the mark was a pun on the *orb* of *Corbold*. This version of his mark is by far the most common, appearing on over 100 pieces of excellent quality, mostly dating from 1565 to 1569.

3

Communion cup *Silver, parcel-gilt*

Norwich; 1565–6; maker's mark of William Cobbold (c.1530–1585/6)
St Mary's Church, Diss, Norfolk

On domed foot with spreading foot with small dentilated borders, rising to a spool-form stem with central knop decorated with punched strokes, and bell-shaped bowl engraved with a central band of arabesques between applied reeded borders

Francis Blomefield, writing in the mid-eighteenth century, recorded that : "At the Reformation, the church plate was sold to Henry, Earl of Sussex, August 15th, 1546 ... I find that they sold all so far, that in 1572 they had only one cup of 23 oz. Wt."[1] In 1572 the churchwardens bought a cover.

H. 7½ in. (19 cm); DIAM. 5¼ in. (13.2 cm);
WEIGHT 18 oz. (560 g)

3

4

Communion cup and paten-cover *Silver-gilt*

*c.*1540 and parts *c.*1568; maker's mark of William Cobbold
(*c.*1530–1585/6)
St Andrew's Church, Norwich

*On spreading foot with a band of profile busts amid foliate
scrolls, on trumpet-shaped stem chased with scrolling acanthus
on a textured ground, with openwork calyx of scrolling leaves,
the deep tapering cylindrical bowl engraved with a band of
alternating plain and matted spiral flutes below a horizontal
band of circles; the domed cover chased with a band of lions'
heads amid scrolling foliage and applied, probably in 1568, with
a spool-form foot, the top engraved* THIS CUPP / TAYNYNG T /
O S ANDRES / PRISHE 1568

Marks: Struck on rim with castle and lion, date letter upper-
case roman A in square punch (Jackson, p. 336, line 1) and
with maker's mark an orb and cross in a lozenge (Levine,
no. 1); also with zigzag assay gouge in three places

Published: Blomefield, vol. 1, p. 28; NA Redenhall, p. 91,
illus. opp. p. 76; *Norwich Silver*, Norwich, p. 11

Exhibited: Norwich Silver, Norwich, 1966, no. 1

1 Norwich Silver, *Norwich*, p. 11.

4

This cup, with decoration in the Renaissance style, is a secular wine or beer goblet which, some time after it was made, was acquired by the church of St Andrew as a communion cup. The spool-form foot to the cover is typical of Elizabethan patens and was clearly inserted when the cup was presented to the church in 1568, probably replacing a figural or ball finial. The cup and the very similar one belonging to Wood Dalling church, no. 5, pose a number of questions regarding origin and silver production in Norwich before the opening of the assay office in 1565.

The form of the cup is unusual. The deep bucket shape of the bowl, with its flat base, is reminiscent of Venetian glass goblets imported into Britain during the reign of Henry VIII. In English Renaissance silver a calyx of rolled openwork acanthus leaves is rare. There are German examples, especially from Nuremberg, but in England, apart from these two cups, the only other one seems to be the Caird Cup, struck with London hallmarks for 1529–30 and a maker's mark resembling a merchant's mark.[1] Similar calices first appear in the designs of Hans Holbein the younger, who arrived in England in 1526 and became "King's Painter" in 1536. One of his drawings of about 1532, done for his friend, the goldsmith Hans of Antwerp, who was then working in London, shows a similar calyx on a covered cup.[2] A virtually identical border of die stamping is on the foot of Robert Morwen's "cruse", or two-handled cup, London, 1533–4, belonging to Corpus Christi College, Oxford.[3]

Given the presence of a Cobbold maker's mark on the rim of the present cup, and the lack of hallmarks, it may be that it was a gift of Cobbold to his own parish church in 1568.[4] But whether Cobbold himself made the cup is open to doubt. The presence of the other, almost identical, cup at Wood Dalling bearing London hallmarks for 1531–2 can be explained in several ways. Both cups could be part of a set made in London in the 1530s, handled by Cobbold as second-hand plate in the 1560s and aquired by both churches as part of the great chalice conversion programme. Another explanation is that Cobbold made the St Andrew's cup himself, using the London-made Wood Dalling example as his model. While both cups are similar, there are sufficient differences in the decoration, especially in the fluting around the bowl, the handling of the chasing and particularly in the dies used to stamp the border around the foot, to suggest two different workshops.[5] If that is the case, when did Cobbold make the St Andrew's cup? Was it made in the years between his freedom in 1552 and the establishment of hallmarking in Norwich in 1565? If so, might he have struck it with his maker's mark, and, subsequently having it in stock again, sold or given it to St Andrew's Church in 1568?

Cup: H: 7½ in. (19 cm); DIAM: 4⅜ in. (11 cm)
Paten-cover: H: 1½ in. (3.8 cm); DIAM: 4½ in. (11.4 cm)

Marks: Struck on rim with maker's mark an orb and cross in a lozenge (Levine, no. 1)

Published: NA Norwich, p. 77, illus.; Oman, *Church Plate*, p. 196, plate 59A

Exhibited: Art Loan, Norwich, 1902, p. 19; *Norwich Silver Plate*, Norwich, 1911, no. 54; *Norwich Silver*, Norwich, 1966, no. 19

1 In the Al-Tajir Collection; sold from the collection of Sir James Caird, Bt., Christie's London, July 14, 1993, lot 117.
2 Öffentliche Kunstsammlungen, Basle.
3 Clifford, fig. 68, p. 67.
4 For biographical details of Cobbold see p. 39.
5 The two cups were examined by me, Nigel Bumphrey, Mary Fewster and Christopher Garibaldi in May 2001 and I am grateful to all of them for their suggestions.

5

Communion cup *Silver-gilt*

London; 1531–2; maker's mark unidentified, possibly a flowerhead

St Andrew's Church, Wood Dalling, Norfolk

Similar to the preceding, but with slightly simplified decoration, the stem and calyx unscrewing from the bowl, the bowl engraved *Wood Dalling* *in* *Norf*

H. 7¼ in. (18.4 cm); DIAM. 4¼ in. (10.7 cm); WEIGHT. 14 OZ. (435 g)

Marks: Struck on foot with leopard's head and date letter Lombardic upper-case O (Jackson, p. 49, column 1, line 13), and with maker's mark

5

6

6

Jug *Silver-gilt, salt-glazed stoneware*

The jug: Frechen (near Cologne), *c.*1560–70
The mounts: Norwich; 1568–9; maker's mark a five-petalled rose
Private Collection through Koopman/Rare Art Ltd.

The bulbous body on spreading foot applied with a rim foot with a band of tongue and dart with a scalloped stiff foliate rim above, the neck with a similarly-scalloped mount engraved with inter-laced bands of arabesques, with box hinge mount decorated with a trellis pattern and surmounted by a cast double dolphin scroll thumb-piece, the domed cover engraved with arabesques and applied with three cast bearded male busts enclosing a baluster finial with foliate calyx

This is the finest of the group of five surviving Norwich-mounted "tigerware" jugs.[1] Rhenish salt-glazed stoneware pots were imported into England in huge quantities and appear to have been the most common drinking vessels used in houses and taverns.[2] They were sometimes "garnished" with silver and were often, as with this example, given a hinged cover. A French visitor to England, Etienne Perlin, writing in 1558, commented that the English "consume great quantities of beer … and do not drink it out of glasses, but from earthen pots with silver handles and covers, and this even in houses of persons of middling fortune". John Gray's probate inventory of 1594 lists "iij lipped potts" (see p. 26). Along with spoons, mounted jugs were the most common items of silver in households below gentry level.

The mounts on this jug show many of the features typical of East Anglian silver of the period, such as the bands of mauresque engraving between zigzag borders. Other features are virtually identical to those found on objects from the Cobbold workshop. The finely finished thumb-piece and die stamped borders are also found on two Cobbold flagons (fig. 11, p. 26) suggesting interchange of components between the two workshops.

H. 9 in. (22.8 cm); W. 4¾ in. (12 cm); D. 4¾ in. (12 cm)

Marks: Struck on rim with castle and lion and date letter upper-case roman D in square punch and with maker's mark (Jackson, p. 336, line 8, marks from this piece illustrated),

maker's mark also struck under foot; interior of cover and under side of foot with zigzag gouge

Provenance: Anonymous sale, Christie's, London, November 23, 1982, E. & C. T. Koopman Ltd.; Brand Inglis Ltd.; private collection

Published: *Norwich Silver*, Norwich, p. 17; Barrett, *Norwich Silver*, illus. p. 60; Clayton, *History*, illus. p. 39, fig. 2

Exhibited: *Norwich Silver*, Norwich, 1966, no. 24, p. 17

1 They include: 1569–70, Peter Peterson (exhibited Norwich, 1966, no. 26), 1571–2, William Cobbold (exhibited How of Edinburgh, London, 1937, no. 9; Norwich, 1966, no. 28; sold Sotheby's, London, July 8, 1986, lot 291 and again from Bewley Court, Lacock, Wilts., house sale, Sotheby's, May 17, 1993, lot 26), *c.*1571–5, Christopher Tanner (Norwich Castle Museum & Art Gallery), and another by the same (private collection).
2 Interestingly, unmounted Rhenish stoneware jugs like these appear to have been used well into the eighteenth century. At Raynham Hall near Fakenham, craftsmen working on William Kent's alterations to the dining room in the late 1720s left under the floor boards a quantity of unused carving, clay pipes and a number of these jugs.

Peter Peterson I (fl.1554–1603)

(Cat. no. 7)

Peter Peterson was the most famous Norwich goldsmith of the Elizabethan period until it was found that the orb-and-cross mark, which appears on the finest Norwich-made plate, had wrongly been attributed to him.

Of Dutch descent, Peterson was born in about 1518, apprenticed to John Basyngham I and admitted free in 1554.[1] He was master in 1565, a warden in 1570 and again in 1587, and chamberlain of the city between 1570 and 1575. The post of chamberlain would have given Peterson access to civic funds for his own use, which may account for his wealth.

The mark of a sun, first linked to Peterson by the late

George Levine, is a rebus punning on the last syllable of Peterson's name. The churchwardens' accounts for St Margaret record under 1565: "pd. To Pet' Peterson, ye Goldesmyth, for making ye communion cuppe, for every owne wourken vj*d*. Sm. xij owc and di vj*s*. Iij*d*…"; the cup, illustrated on p. 15, fig. 3, is struck with the sun in splendour.

The output of Peterson's workshop is not always of the highest quality, as can be seen in the modest and somewhat awkward cup, no. 7, but judging from the numerous bequests in his will dated May 15, 1603,[2] he evidently ran a prosperous workshop, located at what is now no. 3 Castle Street.[3] He had other business interests too and extensive property in the city as well as at Barnham Broome, Barford and Carleton Forehoe.[4]

Peterson's will bequeaths more than forty spoons and a number of mourning rings, all with the motto "Remember Peterson". Most are described as being marked with "the sonne". Peterson's seal was also the sun in splendour and appears attached to a deed of 1588 for tenements in Cutler Row.[5] Peterson leaves to George Birch "my veary good frynd and neighbour":

One silver pott with a cover all gylte with eares, called Hauncepott, graven ypon the covers wth the sonne, the Lion and Castle of Norwich tuch, of my owne making …"

Peterson married twice but appears to have had no children. However, a great-nephew,[6] also Peter, became a goldsmith and was left his great-uncle's tools and lead patterns in the latter's will. Directions for Peterson's burial in St Andrew's Church "where I doe usually sitt" are laid out, with a brass to be set up with the following verse:

I, Peter Peterson, Gentleman, Goldsmith, dead and gone,
Here lieth, buryed under this stone,
As you be nowe soe sometimes was he,
And as he is nowe soe shall you be,
Inclosed in earth his bones doe rest,
His soule wth Christ in Heaven is blest"

Nothing remains of this monument, nor does his portrait, also mentioned in the will.

Peterson's mark appears on nearly fifty pieces of church plate and one tigerware jug.[7]

1 Freemen, Norwich, p. 70.
2 Printed in NA vol. 11.
3 Beecheno, *St Andrew's Parish*, p. 23.
4 Hartop, *Norwich Goldsmiths*, p. 28; see a conveyance of estates in these parishes "late the property of Peter Peterson, goldsmith" in 1610, in the Wodehouse papers NRO/KIM 2L/23–5.
5 Colman Manuscripts, NRO/COL/1/127.
6 I am grateful to Mary Fewster for this information.
7 Barrett, *Norwich Silver*, p. 90.

7

Marks: Struck on rim with castle and lion, date letter upper-case roman C in square punch (Jackson, p. 336, line 1) and with maker's mark a sun in splendour (Levine, no. 6)

Published: NA Taverham, *sub* East Carlton

8

Cup *Silver*

Norwich; dated 1623; maker's mark a bird
St Margaret's Church, Morton, Norfolk

On spreading foot rising to a tapering baluster stem and everted bowl pricked around the outside ANO 1623 FOR YE TOWNE OF MORTON AND HELMINGHAM

7

Communion cup *Silver*

Norwich; 1567–8; maker's mark of Peter Peterson I
(fl. 1554–1603)
St Mary's Church, East Carlton, Norfolk

On double spool foot (utilizing a paten-cover, probably added at a later date) and everted bowl engraved + THE TOWNE OF ESTE CARLTON 1568 *within ruled zigzag borders*

H. 6 in. (15.2 cm); DIAM. 3⅝ in. (9.2 cm);
WEIGHT 5 OZ. (155 g)

8

While this secular wine cup is typical of the early seventeenth century, its marks present problems in dating. The castle and lion mark is the version found alone or in conjunction with a maker's mark on a small number of pieces that stylistically can be dated between 1590 and 1630. For example, a silver-gilt seal-top spoon in a private collection, struck with the same town mark (characterized by distinctive rustication in the central portion of the castle), is prick dated 1614. The meaning of the incuse letter G on this cup is unclear. Could it be that Commander How's suggestion, made in the 1940s, that another cycle of date letters was in use in the twenty years up to the re-establishment of date letters in 1624 is correct? "Many of the spoons which have been found bearing these marks [i.e., the 1624–42 date-letter cycle] might equally well be twenty years earlier than the date they appear to be from Jackson."[1] If this is indeed the case, the date 1623 pricked on this cup could be explained. The same three marks appear on the secular cup and cover of St Peter Hungate, Norwich, which should now also be dated to the early 1620s.

H. 7⅝ in. (9.4 cm); DIAM. 3 in. (7.5 cm); WEIGHT 4 oz. (124 g)

Marks: struck on rim with castle and lion (Jackson, p. 337, line 7), maker's mark (ibid., line 14) and with unidentified incuse upper-case roman G

1 How, "Constructive Criticism", p. 153.

9

9

Seal-top spoon *Silver*

Norwich; 1632–3; maker's mark of Richard Shipden
(fl. 1610–1638)
Private Collection

With fig-shaped bowl and with slightly tapering hexagonal stem and fluted baluster finial; engraved on top with initials 16?33 over IN over MB

Richard Shipden was evidently a respected member of the goldsmiths' guild but his mark, a rebus of a ship,[1] has only come down to us on five spoons, four of them seal tops.[2] He served as warden of the company five times between 1629 and 1636,[3] but it appears from the bequests in his will, which total nearly £1,500, and the extensive property holdings that it mentions, that he had made most of his money in land

speculation and possibly banking.[4] He was buried in 1638 in St Peter Parmentergate Church, Norwich.

L. 6⅝ in. (17 cm)

Marks: Struck on bowl with crowned rose and on back of stem with castle and lion, date letter upper-case roman I (Jackson, p. 337, line 10) and maker's mark (Levine, no. 17)

Provenance: Said to have been found in a house in Norwich, anonymous sale, Bonham's, Bury St Edmunds, December 16, 2002, lot 149, private collection

1 Rebus, or punning, marks remained popular well into the seventeenth century. Another maker's mark found on several objects from the 1630s is of a bird emerging from a pot, and it has been put forward by Wynyard Wilkinson that this may be the mark of William Kettleburgh, free 1634.
2 The fifth is a slip-top with mother-of-pearl bowl, 1632–3, exhibited *Norwich Silver*, Norwich, 1966, no. 49.
3 Barrett, *Norwich Goldsmiths*, pp. 92–3.
4 Levine, "Norwich Goldsmiths' Wills", p. 488.

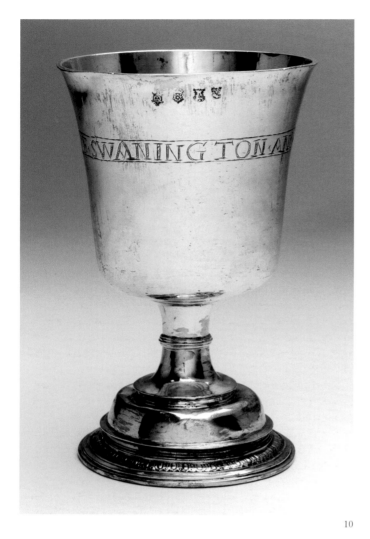

cup is perhaps explained by the reuse of an Elizabethan foot from an earlier cup.

H. 6¼ in. (15.9 cm); DIAM. 3⅝ in. (9.2 cm); WEIGHT 9 oz. 3 dwt. (284 g)

Marks: Struck on rim with castle and lion, crowned rose, date letter upper-case roman Q (Jackson, p. 337, line 18) and with maker's mark (Levine, no. 26)

11

Seal-top spoon *Silver-gilt*

Norwich; 1641–2; maker's mark a pelican in her piety
The Ticktum Collection

With fig-shaped bowl and with slightly hexagonal stem and fluted baluster finial; engraved on top with initials SLF *over* SF *over* 1641

Two other seal tops spoons by this maker are recorded,[1] all of the highest quality, as well as an apostle spoon.

L. 6⅝ in. (16.7 cm)

Marks: Struck on the bowl with crowned rose and on back of stem with castle and lion, date letter upper-case roman S (Jackson, p. 337, line 20) and with maker's mark (Levine, no. 26)

10

10

Cup *Silver*

Norwich; 1639–40; maker's mark a pelican in her piety
St Margaret's Church, Swannington, Norfolk

On high domed cover with an outer band of egg and dart, rising to a spool-form stem with small knop and deep flaring bowl, engraved FOR THE TOWN OF SWANINGTON ANO. DOMNE 1639 *within ruled borders*

This maker's mark appears in conjunction with Norwich marks on a dozen pieces dating between 1624 and 1641, including a magnificent secular silver-gilt cup and cover of 1635–6, richly chased with cockatrices amid foliage, belonging to the church of St Lawrence, Beeston (fig. 12), and on several spoons (see no. 11). The awkwardness of this

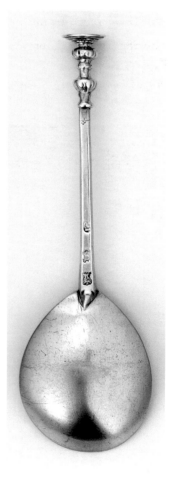

11

Provenance: Henry Levine Ltd., Norwich, from whom purchased by Christine Winfield in 1970, The Winfield Collection, Bonhams & Brooks, London, March 6, 2001, lot 87, the Ticktum Collection

1 The first of 1624–5, dated 1625, John H. F. Walter Collection, sold Sotheby's London, July 2, 1954, lot 159 (bt. How), Gerald S. Sanders, Norwich Castle Museum & Art Gallery; the other of 1637–8, dated 1637, sold from the same collection, lot 156 (bt. G. N. Barrett). A fragment of another spoon, lacking its finial but, from the presence of pricked initials C over IM on the back of the bowl, evidently once an apostle spoon, was found in a garden in Norwich a few years ago. It is now in the Ticktum Collection.

12

Paten *Silver*

Norwich: 1641–2; maker's mark a D in a shaped square punch

St Peter Southgate Church, Norwich

Plain circular with flat rim

This appears to be the only recorded instance of this maker's mark.

DIAM. 3⅞ in. (9.7 cm)

12

Marks: Struck on rim with castle and lion, crowned rose, date letter upper-case roman S, and with maker's mark D in a shaped punch (Jackson, p. 337, line 23, marks from this piece illustrated)

Published: NA, Norwich, p. 108, where Canon Manning mistook the maker's mark for the date letter for 1627–8; Jackson, p. 337, line 23

Timothy Skottowe (fl. *c.*1617–1645)

(Cat. no. 13)

Timothy Skottowe is one of the best-known silversmiths of the early seventeenth century, partly because he was a prominent figure in Civil War Norwich, and also because a wide variety of marks similar to his have, over the years, been erroneously attributed to him (see p. 71). Descended from a Norfolk minor gentry family, Skottowe was the son of a Norwich alderman, Richard Skottowe.[1] He was admitted free by patrimony on March 29, 1617 and early in his career took as an apprentice Richard Cobbold,[2] probably the grandson of William Cobbold.

Skottowe served as warden of the company eleven times between 1624 and 1642,[3] the year that the date-letter system was abandoned. By then, England was fully in the grip of civil war and in that year Skottowe was appointed collector of the plate and coin being delivered up at Norwich, Lynn, Thetford and Yarmouth to provide loans for the Parliamentary cause, and given the task of melting the plate and coin into ingots.[4] One receipt signed by Skottowe, to Sir John Potts for his £100 worth of plate, survives in the Tanner MSS.[5] The following year he helped raise a hundred men for Cromwell, but he did not entirely agree with the way events were turning, for later that year he refused, along with Sir Thomas Browne and others, to subscribe to "The Subscription towards the Regaining of Newcastle".[6]

When Skottowe died in 1645, he left an estate of over £800.[7] Among the many bequests is the legacy of £1 to Daniel Eynsworth, then aged about 70, who had been a prominent goldsmith and with whom Skottowe had served as joint warden on several occasions.

1 Levine, p. 298.
2 Freeman, Norwich, p. 70.
3 Barrett, *Norwich Silver*, p. 93.
4 Ketton-Cremer, p. 64.
5 Bodleian Library, MS Tanner 64, ff. 8, 9.
6 Levine, p. 298.
7 Levine, "Norwich Goldsmiths' Wills", p. 489; see also Skottowe, p. 13.

13

Spout cup *Silver*

Norwich; 1642–3; maker's mark of Timothy Skottowe
(fl. 1617–1645)

The Trustees of the Victoria & Albert Museum, London

*Tapering cylindrical with tubular scroll handle and curved spout
at right-angles; the flat hinged cover with scroll handle formed of
a strip between two scrolled plates, the front later engraved with
a coat of arms within plume mantling and surmounted by a crest
of a tree*

The engraving on the front of this pot is later. The crossed
plumes are typical of the 1660s (see fig. 14), while the coat of
arms and crest are clearly even much later than these and
were probably added in the nineteenth century.

The form of this spout cup, with its large scrolling thumb-
piece, follows London-made tankards of the period such as
the example of 1635–6, maker's mark RS, in the Assheton
Bennett Collection, Manchester City Art Gallery.

H. 4³⁄₈ in. (11.1 cm); w. 4⁷⁄₈ in. (12.5 cm);
WEIGHT 8 oz. 10 dwt. (264 g)

Heraldry: The coat of arms can be blazoned *quarterly or and
azure* and was borne by the Fastolfe or Falstolfe family of
Norfolk and Suffolk, but the crest, *out of a tun, a tree*, is
similar to that borne by the Servington family of Devon.

Marks: Struck on side by spout and on top of cover with castle
and lion, crowned rose, date letter upper-case roman T
(Jackson, p. 337, line 24) and maker's mark (Levine, no. 19)

Provenance: Victoria & Albert Museum, Gift of L. C. Price,
1920 (M84-1920)

Published: English Silver, Ontario, C15; Oman, plate 52;
Clayton, *Dictionary*, illus. fig. 566; Glanville, *Tudor and Early
Stuart*, p. 438, no. 59

Exhibited: English Silver, Ontario, 1958, no. C15

13

14

14

Beaker *Silver*

Norwich; *c.*1645; unidentified maker
Private Collection

Wide tapering cylindrical on moulded foot, engraved with a broad band of stylized foliage, engraved with the initials HFM *and later, probably in the nineteenth century, with initials* MA/EB

H. 3 in. (7.6 cm); DIAM. 2¾ in. (7 cm)

Marks: Struck four times under base with castle and lion (Jackson, p. 338, line 1)

The Haslewood family (fl. *c.*1625–1740)
(Cat. nos. 15–33)

The business operated by three generations of the Haslewood family in Norwich between about 1625 and 1740 produced some of the best provincial seventeenth-century plate. The family has been the subject of research by the late Geoffrey Barrett, who was the first writer to separate the mark attributions of Arthur I from those of Arthur II.[1]

Arthur Haslewood I was born in 1593[2] and was apprenticed to Daniel Eynsworth. He was admitted a freeman on May 30, 1625[3] and early on appears to have established himself as a worthy member of the guild, for he served as warden in 1628, 1629 and 1640. He was not rich, however, for the fine of five shillings levied on him by the London company when they visited Norwich in 1635 was not collected by them "being fully informed of the povity of the aforesaid Arthur Haselwood by some well knowing his estate taking into consideration the great loss he sustained by the breaking of all his plate and wares according to the trial".[4] He lived in the parish St Peter Mancroft but when he died, on March 25 14, 1671, he was buried in St Andrew's Church, to which parish the family had moved after 1668.[5]

No more than a dozen pieces, including four items of church plate, survive from the elder Haslewood's workshop.

Arthur Haslewood II was admitted free by patrimony on March 26, 1661[6] and he (or his father, who may by then have retired) shortly afterwards subscribed five shillings to the gift offered by the city to King Charles II.[7] He was a councillor for St Peter Mancroft between 1663 and 1668 and after that date appears to have moved to the house and shop on the south side of the Cockey, a ditch that ran along what is now Little London Street. The family lived there, next to Mr Chase the printer, until 1740. Haslewood died, aged forty-six, on November 14, 1684 and was buried in St Andrew's Church, where he had been churchwarden, leaving a widow, Elizabeth, and three sons and five daughters. Arthur II's

Fig. 24 The tombstone of Arthur Haslewood II, his widow Elizabeth and their son Arthur Haslewood III in the floor of the south aisle of St Andrew's Church, Norwich. *Photograph by John Adamson*

mark occurs on more than seventy-five objects, of which forty-six pieces of church plate.[8]

Elizabeth Haslewood, widow of Arthur II, was the daughter of Robert Wood, gentleman, of Brooke. At the time of her husband's death, her eldest son Robert was already apprenticed in another trade, and her second son Thomas was at Corpus Christi College, Cambridge[9] and was later to take Holy Orders. Her youngest son, Arthur, at the age of 11 may already have started to help in the silversmiths' workshop and so, perhaps with the expectation that in a few years he would be able to run the shop himself, Elizabeth, following the example of many women of the period, assumed control of the business and began to use her own maker's mark, an EH crowned. There were no doubt orders pending and it is an indication of her standing in the community that, only two months after her husband's death, the Mayor's Court Book for January 14 records: "Mrs. Haslewood to be paid 42/6 for gilding the sword".[10] The following year the London company searchers came to Norwich and fined her £13 5s for substandard goods (Thomas Havers and James Daniell also were fined).[11] Evidently her business continued to prosper, for there survive nearly fifty pieces bearing her mark. On December 29, 1689 the *Town Book* of Brooke, her birthplace, records: "Paid Mrs. Hazlewood for mending the Communion plate 5/6".[12]

Elizabeth Haslewood died January 22, 1715, aged 71, and now lies under the same tombstone as her husband. Her will, after various bequests to her children, leaves the residue of her estate to her son Arthur on condition that he maintains her daughter Elizabeth for the rest of her life, suggesting that she may have suffered from illness or a disability.[13] One of the witnesses to the will was the silversmith James Daniell.

Arthur Haslewood III was admitted a freeman on July 1, 1702. He appears to have worked with his mother in the shop in Cockey Lane for he is named there as being fined by the London company searchers for substandard plate in 1703, 1705 and again in 1719, showing that at least some plate continued to be made there well after the end of official hall-marking in Norwich.[14] Elizabeth Haslewood's will mentions her "charges of plate" suggesting, however, that she carried on as owner, or at any rate manager, of the business until her death. Arthur III was churchwarden of St Andrew's in 1717 and died in 1740 and was buried with his parents in St Andrew's church. No mark has been identified for him, and it is unlikely that he had one.

1 See Barrett, "Haslewood Family"; the same article appeared with some revisions in NA, vol. 33, pp. 318–20.

2 Levine, p. 298.

3 Freemen, Norwich, p. 70.
4 Barrett, *Norwich Silver*, p. 36.
5 Beecheno, *St Andrew's Church*.
6 Freemen, Norwich, p. 70.
7 Barrett, *Norwich Silver*, p. 86.
8 Ibid., p. 86.
9 *Norfolk Genealogy*, vol. 17, p. 98.
10 Rye, *Court Books*, p. 421.
11 Barrett, *Norwich Silver*, p. 87.
12 Levine, p. 299.
13 NRO/NCC Wills 325 Melchior.
14 See also "An account of plate belonging to Thomas Seaman esq. weighed and valued by Arthur Haslewood at £187" in the Nelthorpe papers in the Lincolnshire Archives (NEL IV/22/5).

15

Seal-top spoon *Silver, parcel-gilt*

Norwich; 1638–9; maker's mark of Arthur Haslewood I (1593–1671)

Private Collection

With fig-shaped bowl and with slightly hexagonal stem and fluted baluster finial; engraved on top with initials RW over AM over 1645

L. 7⅛ in. (18 cm)

Marks: Struck on the bowl with crowned rose and on back of stem with castle and lion, date letter upper-case roman P, and crowned rose over the lap joint (Jackson, p. 337, line 18) and with maker's mark (Levine, no. 20)

15

16

17

16

Beaker *Silver*

Norwich; *c*.1650; maker's mark of Arthur Haslewood I
(1593–1671)

Private Collection

*Tapering cylindrical on moulded foot, the slightly tapering sides
engraved with a broad band of stylized foliage, engraved under
the base with the initials WL*

H. 3¾ in. (9.5 cm); DIAM. 2¾ in. (7 cm)

Marks: Struck four times under base with maker's mark
(cf. Jackson, p. 338, line 3)

17

Stump-end spoon *Silver*

Norwich; *c*.1665–1670; maker's mark of Arthur
Haslewood II (1638–1684)

Private Collection

*With egg-shaped bowl and flat stem, with rat-tail; the back of the
terminal pricked* TI *over* IK *over* 85

L. 7⅞ in. (18.6 cm)

Marks: Struck on reverse of stem with castle and lion, a
crown (Jackson, p. 338, line 8) and with maker's mark
(Levine, no. 20); the bowl struck with a rose

Provenance: The Cook Collection, sale, Woolley & Wallis,
Salisbury, October 24, 2003, lot 1077, private collection

18

Trefid spoon *Silver*

Norwich; *c*.1665–70; maker's mark of Arthur Haslewood II (1638–1684)

Private Collection

With egg-shaped bowl and flat stem, with rat-tail; the front of the terminal pricked TG *over* WI

L. 7⅛ in (18.9 cm)

Marks: Struck on reverse of stem with a rose and a crown (Jackson, p. 338, line 8); and with maker's mark (Levine, no. 20); the bowl struck with castle and lion

Provenance: Anonymous sale, Christie's, London, July 10, 1913, lot 121; anonymous sale, Christie's, London, April 24, 1917, lot 47; Reuben Levine, Norwich, sale, Christie's, London, May 14, 1928, lot 62 (bt. Turner); The Griffin Collection, sale, Phillips, London, July 20, 2001, lot 482; private collection

Published: Park Lane, London no. 320

Exhibited: Park Lane, London, 1929, no. 320

19

Tankard *Silver*

Norwich; *c*.1660–80; maker's mark of Arthur Haslewood II (1638–1684)

Private Collection

Slightly tapering cylindrical on moulded foot, the flat hinged domed cover with bifurcated thumb-piece, with tubular scroll handle terminating in a semicircle; the top of the handle pricked with the initials T *over* IM

There are three tankards recorded by Arthur Haslewood II.[1] Stylistically, with its small mouldings and proportions, this tankard can be dated to the 1660s or 70s; the same punches were used by Haslewood on spoons of the early trefid type, one of which is dated 1669. There is a similar thumb-piece on an Elizabeth Haslewood tankard of 1691–2.

L. 6¼ in (15.9 cm); W. 7½ in. (19 cm); D. 4⅛ in. (10.4 cm); WEIGHT 23 oz. 2 dwt. (718 g)

Marks: Struck on body by handle and on top of cover with castle and lion, a rose and a crown (Jackson, p. 338, line 8), and with maker's mark (Levine, no. 21)

Provenance: John H. F. Walter JP (1847–1927), Drayton Hall, Norwich, The Walter Collection, sale, Sotheby's, London, May 20, 1954, lot 156 (bt. Willson), Walter H. Willson Ltd., London, 1955; anonymous sale, Christie's, London, March 20, 1963, lot 107; Spink & Son Ltd., London, 1977; anonymous sale, Bonhams, London, July 23, 2004, lot 100, private collection

Published: Norwich Silver Plate, Norwich, p. 9, no. 24; *Antique Dealers' Fair*, London, p. 85; *Grosvenor House Antiques Fair*, London, p. 54

Exhibited: Norwich Silver Plate, Norwich, 1911, no. 24, lent by John H. F. Walter; *Antique Dealers' Fair*, London, 1955, exhibited by Walter H. Willson Ltd.; *Grosvenor House Antiques Fair*, London, 1977, exhibited by Spink & Son Ltd.

1 See no. 20. The third is similar to the present example with the addition of an engraved coat of arms (exhibited *Norwich Silver*, Norwich, 1966, cat. no. 90).

18

19

20

Tankard *Silver*

Norwich; *c*.1675–80; maker's mark of Arthur Haslewood II
(1638–1684)

Collection of Mrs Véronique Peck, Los Angeles

*Of slightly tapering cylindrical form on spreading moulded foot,
the lower part of the body chased with vertical alternating
acanthus and pounced water leaves, the flat hinged domed cover
with lion-form thumb-piece, with tubular scroll handle pierced
with thistles at the shoulder and applied with a rat-tail
terminating with a ring, the front engraved with a lozenge of
arms within plume mantling, engraved under the base with
later (probably late nineteenth-century) coat of arms and
baron's coronet*

This hitherto unpublished tankard is the most impressive
and elaborate Norwich-made example to survive. Its lion-
form thumb-piece is unique in Norwich silver, although
examples made in London are not uncommon. The use of
animal-form thumb-pieces and feet for tankards appears to
have been introduced by immigrant craftsmen in the 1650s,[1]
although the examples with London marks from the 1670s
have the marks of a number of different makers including
those of the Englishmen Thomas Jenkins and William
Jennings, but both of whom are known to have "covered" the
work of "strangers".[2] Most of the London-made examples
with lion-form thumb-pieces and chased vertical acanthus
leaves around the body, like the Haslewood example, are of
large size and bear the maker's mark TC with dolphin and
fleur-de-lis, such as the one of 1678–9 at Oriel College,
Oxford,[3] or the mark IA in beaded oval.[4] Interestingly, the
Oriel tankard also has bolection moulding around the base,

which features on the Norwich example and was a regular
feature on silver from the Haslewood workshop.

It is curious why the arms engraved on the front, which
appear to be contemporary with the tankard's manufacture,
are depicted in the traditional lozenge used to denote a
spinster, given the masculine scale and weight of the piece.
Small tankards, under four inches high, have often been
described as "ladies' tankards",[5] but this may underline the
fact that large tankards of this size were essentially for display, often given or bequeathed as commemorative pieces.

The Herald's Visitation to Suffolk in 1561 confirmed to
the family of Cooke of Great Linstead the following arms:
*Or a chevron engrailed Gules between three cinquefoils Azure
on a chief Gules a lion passant Argent*,[6] and the arms appear on
monuments at Beccles, Assington and Ipswich.[7] The same
arms were also used by the Cooke family of Washingford
House, Bergh Apton, Norfolk,[8] appearing there in the
church on the monument of Frances Cooke (d. 1826), which
appears to reuse a late seventeenth-century coat of arms.

It is the Cookes of Bergh Apton who may provide a
possible candidate for the original owner of this tankard.
Richard Cooke of Bergh Apton, gentleman, died there and
was buried on August 19, 1684 leaving, in addition to four
sons, a daughter, Elizabeth (b. 1654), to whom he left "One
Hundred pounds Fifty pounds [*sic*] thereof to be paid unto
her within One halfe yeare next after the day of her marrige
And in Case Shee doth not marry then three pounds to be
paid yearely during her life …"[9]

H. 8 in. (20.3 cm); w. 8 in. (20.3 cm); D. 6⅜ in (16.2 cm);
WEIGHT 37 OZ. (1150 g)

Heraldry: The arms engraved on the front are those of an
unmarried lady of the Cooke family of Linstead, Suffolk and
Bergh Apton, Norfolk; the nineteenth-century arms
engraved under the base are those of Willoughby.

Marks: Struck on body by handle and on top of cover with
castle and lion, a rose and a crown (Jackson, p. 338, line 7)
and with maker's mark (Levine no. 21)

Provenance: Mrs Oscar Johnson, St Louis, Missouri, sale,
Sotheby's, New York, October 13, 1984, lot 170; Gregory
Peck, Los Angeles, California

20 (detail)

20 (marks)

20

1 Hartop, *Fogg*, no. 16.
2 Hartop, *Huguenot Legacy*, pp. 251–2.
3 Moffatt, p. 40, plate xx; Clifford, *Oxford*, p. 87, where she notes that it holds a gallon.
4 One of 1677–8 sold anonymously, Christie's, London, March 21, 1962, lot 134.
5 For example the London-made example of 1674–5 in the Fogg Art Museum, Harvard University, 1949.114.35.
6 *Harleian Society*, NS, vol. 3 (1984), pp. 324–5.
7 Reynolds and Machlachlan, *sub* Cooke.
8 East Anglian Pedigrees, NRS, vol. 13, pp. 44–6.
9 Quoted in Geoffrey I. Kelly: *Washingford House, Bergh Apton, a History* (unpublished bound typescript, Norfolk Heritage Centre, 2002).

21

Beaker *Silver*

Norwich; *c*.1690; maker's mark of Elizabeth Haslewood (fl. 1684–?1715)

Lent by Her Majesty The Queen

Of plain slightly flaring form on moulded rim foot; the side pricked IT *over* FH

This beaker may date from before the introduction of the date-letter cycle in 1688, or it may be that the date letter was omitted and the crowned rose struck twice in error.

H. 3½ in. (9 cm); DIAM. 3 in. (7.6 cm); WEIGHT 3 OZ. 15 dwt. (116 g)

Marks: Struck under base with castle and lion and twice with crowned rose (Jackson, p. 339, fig. 2) and with maker's mark (Levine, no. 22)

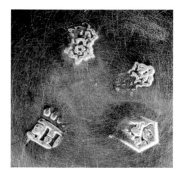

Provenance: Presented to Her Majesty The Queen by Mr F. G. Jackson, Vice-chairman of Norfolk County Council, on behalf of the council, at the opening of the new county hall on May 23, 1968, The Royal Collection

Published: Eastern Evening News, May 24, 1968, "Queen Given City Silver", p. 20

21

22

22

Tobacco box *Silver*

Norwich; apparently 1697–8; maker's mark of Elizabeth Haslewood (fl. 1684–?1715)

The National Museum of Women in the Arts, Washington D.C.

Of oval form with push-on cover pricked on the interior with the initials TB *and engraved (c.1750) on the top with a coat of arms within foliate scrolls surmounted by a crest of a wyvern's head*

The *Norwich Gazette* of September 15–23, 1710, records:

> Lately lost an Oval Silver Snuff-Box, weighing about 3 Ounces, the Gilt within Side a little wore off. Whoever carries the same to Mr. Rich. Waiffe, at his Coffee-house in Norwich, shall have 15s Reward, without asking any Questions

H. 7/8 in. (2.3 cm); W. 3¾ in. (9.5 cm); D. 3 in. (7.6 cm); WEIGHT 4 oz. 15 dwt. (148 g)

Heraldry: The arms and crest are those of Gedding, Norfolk

Marks: Struck on interior of cover and side with crowned rose (Jackson, p. 339, fig. 3) and with maker's mark (Levine, no. 22), the side also with traces of castle and lion and a date letter, possibly the K for 1697–8

Provenance: Geoffrey Barrett Collection; anonymous sale [G. Barrett], Christie's, London, April 27/28, 1983, lot 189, Nancy Valentine, New York, Lorraine and Oliver R. Grace, Long Island, The National Museum of Women in the Arts (acquired in 1989)

Published: Barrett, *Norwich Silver*, p. 50; Glanville and Goldsborough, pp. 10, 112, 166, illustrated plate 86

Exhibited: Norwich Silver, Norwich, 1966, no. 131, lent anonymously

23

Two-handled cup *Silver*

Norwich; 1689–90; maker's mark of Elizabeth Haslewood (fl. 1684–?1715)

Private Collection, Australia

Of circular form on flat base with slightly flaring sides, with two cast foliate scroll handles; one side pricked AG *over* AA *and the other side engraved, probably early in the eighteenth century, with the initials* I*S

This small cup appears to be the only surviving Norwich example with sand-cast foliate scroll handles.

H. 2¼ in. (6 cm); W. 4¾ in. (12 cm); D. 3 in. (7.6 cm)

23

Marks: Struck under base with castle and lion, crowned rose, date letter lower-case gothic b (Jackson, p. 339, line 2) and maker's mark (Levine, no. 22)

Provenance: Sir Peter Wills, Bt., sale, Christie's, London, November 9, 1994, lot 205, J. H. Bourdon-Smith Ltd., London, private collection, Australia

Published: Barrett, *Norwich Silver*, p. 51

24

Beaker *Silver*

Norwich; 1696–7; maker's mark of Elizabeth Haslewood (fl. 1684–?1715)
Private Collection

Of plain slightly flaring form on moulded rim foot; the underside engraved B over IA

H. 3½ in. (9 cm); DIAM. 3 in. (7.6 cm);
WEIGHT 6 oz. 6 dwt. (102 g)

Marks: Struck under base with castle and lion, crowned rose, date letter upper case roman I (Jackson, p. 339, fig. 2, these marks photographed) and maker's mark (Levine, no. 22)

24

Provenance: Reuben Levine, Norwich, sale, "Old Norwich Plate", Christie's, London, May 14, 1928, lot 45 (bt. Crichton); "Property of a Gentleman", Sotheby's, London, July 18, 1968, lot 76 (as 1697); anonymous sale, Phillips, London, November 4, 1994, lot 136, private collection

Published: Barrett, *Norwich Silver*, p. 50

25

Cannon-handled spoon *Silver*

Norwich; 1697–8; maker's mark of Elizabeth Haslewood (fl. 1684–?1715)
Private Collection, United States

Of large size, with deep oval bowl and long rat-tail applied to the reverse, the imposing long tapering cylindrical stem surmounted by a knop finial; the back of the bowl engraved (c.1800) with a crest of a wyvern or gryphon's head engorged, battlemented and chained

This is the largest recorded Norwich-made spoon. One other cannon-handled example is known, with the maker's mark of Thomas Havers and the crowned rose mark, measuring 12 inches in length.[1] It is now in the collection of Norwich Castle Museum & Art Gallery.

L. 16 in. (40.7 cm)

Marks: struck on interior of bowl with castle and lion, crowned rose, date letter upper-case roman K (Jackson, p. 339, line 14) and with maker's mark (Levine, no. 22)

Provenance: Geoffrey Barrett Collection; Anonymous sale [G. N. Barrett], Christie's, London, March 27, 1985, lot 189; private collection

Published: Norwich Silver, Norwich, p. 35; Barrett, *Norwich Silver,* p. 54

Exhibited: Norwich Silver, Norwich, 1966, no. 124, lent anonymously

1 Barrett, *Norwich Silver,* p. 54.

25

26

26

Tumbler cup[1] *Silver*

Norwich; 1697–8; maker's mark of Elizabeth Haslewood (fl. 1684–?1715)
The Albert Collection

Circular with curved base engraved with the initials SB

Very few Norwich tumbler cups are known, although another of the same date and by the same maker has the engraved initials MEN (cat. no. 27).

The hammered construction is quite apparent in this tumbler cup for two reasons. First, because it was not finished to the same degree as would have obtained in a first-class London workshop. Second, the surface has not been abraded through overuse and vigorous polishing. It is also worth noting that fire-marks, or fire-stain, resulting from incomplete annealing and finishing, can be seen on the underside. The slight greying of the silver is due to this process during the manufacture. Where the base has been slightly worn at its centre, the fire-stain is absent.

H. 2 in. (5.7 cm); DIAM. 3 in. (7.6 cm);
WEIGHT 3 oz. 19 dwt. (123 g)

Marks: Struck under base with castle and lion, crowned rose, date letter upper-case roman K (Jackson, p. 339, line 14) and with maker's mark (Levine, no. 22)

Provenance: John H. F. Walter (1847–1927), Drayton Hall, Norwich, The Walter Collection, sale, Sotheby's, London, May 20, 1954, lot 149, (sold with cat. no. 27, bt. S. Lewis); the Albert Collection

Published: Queen Charlotte's Loan, London, p. 72, no. 611; Barrett, *Norwich Silver*, p. 50; Butler, p. 137, no. 47;

Exhibited: Queen Charlotte's Loan, London, 1929, no. 611, lent by the Executors of the late John H. F. Walter

1 This catalogue entry by Robin Butler is from *The Albert Collection* (2004), p. 137, and is reproduced here by kind permission.

27

Tumbler cup *Silver*

Norwich; 1697–7; maker's mark of Elizabeth Haslewood (fl. 1684–?1715)

Private Collection, United States

Circular with curved base engraved with the initials E *over* NM *over* 1701

H. 2⅛ in. (6 cm); DIAM. 3 in. (7.6 cm); WEIGHT 5 OZ. 12 dwt. (174 g)

Marks: Struck under base with castle and lion, crowned rose, date letter upper-case roman K (Jackson, p. 339, line 14) and maker's mark (Levine, no. 22)

Provenance: John H. F. Walter (1847–1927), Drayton Hall, Norwich, The Walter Collection, sale, Sotheby's, London, May 20, 1954, lot 149 (sold with cat. no. 26, bt. S. Lewis); Charles Croydon; Geoffrey Barrett Collection; Anonymous sale [G. Barrett],

27

Christie's, London, April 27/28, 1983, lot 188; private collection

Published: Norwich Silver Plate, Norwich, no. 26; *Norwich Silver*, Norwich, p. 36; Holland, illus. p. 51; Barrett, *Norwich Silver*, p. 50

Exhibited: Norwich Silver Plate, Norwich, 1911, no. 26, lent by John H. F. Walter; *Norwich Silver*, Norwich, 1966, no. 130, lent anonymously

28

Small trefid spoon *Silver*

Norwich; 1697–8; maker's mark of Elizabeth Haslewood (fl. 1684–?1715)

The Ticktum Collection

With egg-shaped bowl and ribbed rat-tail; the reverse of the notched terminal pricked I *over* PM *over* 1699

Of exceptionally small size, this spoon may have been intended for a child.

L. 5½ in. (14 cm)

Mark: Struck on back of stem with castle and lion, crowned rose, date letter upper-case roman K (Jackson, p. 339, line 14) and with maker's mark (Levine, no. 22)

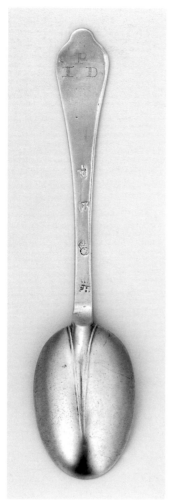

28   29

29

Wavy-end spoon *Silver*

Norwich; 1697–8; maker's mark of Elizabeth Haslewood (fl. 1684–?1715)

The Ticktum Collection

With egg-shaped bowl and wavy end terminal the reverse of which is pricked P *over* ID

L. 7⅞ in. (20 cm)

Marks: Struck on back of stem with castle and lion, crowned rose, date letter upper-case roman K (Jackson, p. 339, line 14) and with maker's mark (Levine, no. 22)

30

Communion cup and paten-cover *Silver*

Norwich; dated 1697–8; maker's mark of Elizabeth Haslewood (fl. 1684–?1715)

St Mary's Church, Colkirk, Norfolk

The cup with deep cylindrical bowl with slightly flaring lip, the cylindrical stem with moulded girdle on domed spreading foot; the paten-cover with spool-form foot; both engraved Colkirke Sanct Maria in Commitat Norff Añ Dō 1700

Work from the Haslewood workshop is characterized by the fine calligraphy of the inscriptions. Unlike the "leopard's

30

30

31

Trefid spoon *Silver*

Norwich; probably 1684–1688, or after 1697; maker's mark of Elizabeth Haslewood (fl. 1684–?1715)

Private Collection

With egg-shaped bowl and flat stem, with rat-tail

L. 8⅛ in. (20.5 cm)

Marks: Struck on reverse of stem with maker's mark (Levine, no. 22)

32

Snuffbox *Silver*

Norwich; *c.*1700–1710; maker's mark of Elizabeth Haslewood (fl. 1684–?1715)

The Ticktum Collection

Of shallow rectangular form with canted corners and with long hinged cover, engraved with borders of circles and foliate scrolls

H. ½ in. (1.2 cm); W. 2½ in. (6.3 cm); D. 1¾ in. (4.4 cm)

31

Mark: Struck on interior of body with maker's mark (Levine, no. 22)

33

Snuffbox *Silver*

Norwich; *c.*1700–1710; maker's mark of Elizabeth Haslewood (fl. 1684–?1715)

The Ticktum Collection

Shell-shaped with straight sides and hinged slightly domed cover engraved with foliage, fruit, a wild mask and two winged cherub heads, engraved on the side of the interior with the initials TW

head and fleur-de-lis" workshop which used pricking almost exclusively, it is clear that the Haslewoods employed a skilled engraver (see also the quality of the decorative engraving on the two snuffboxes nos. 32 and 33).

The cup: H. 7 in. (17.9 cm); DIAM. 4 in. (10 cm)
The paten-cover: H. 1¼ in. (3.2 cm); DIAM. 5⅛ in. (13 cm)

Marks: Struck on rim and on underside rim of paten with castle and lion, crowned rose, date letter upper-case roman K (Jackson, p. 339, fig. 3) and maker's mark (Levine, no. 22)

Published: NA Elmham, *sub* Colkirk

32

33

H. ¾ in. (2 cm); W. 3⅛ in. (8 cm); D. 2⅜ in. (6 cm)

Mark: Struck on interior of body with maker's mark (Levine, no. 22)

Provenance: Anonymous sale, Keys, Aylsham, March 11, 1998, lot 997, the Ticktum Collection

Thomas Havers (fl. *c*.1674–1732)

(Cat. nos. 34–40)

One of the most prolific workshops in Norwich was that attached to the shop of Thomas Havers, situated on the Market Place. Related to a landowning family who had lived at Thelveton Hall near Diss since the early sixteenth century,[1] Havers purchased his freedom on September 21, 1674.[2] In 1686 he was fined £26 14s by the London company wardens for having substandard silver and had £19 1s 3d worth of silver broken,[3] and was fined again in 1703 and 1707. He served as alderman from 1700, was elected sheriff in 1701, and mayor in 1708.[4]

Havers has achieved notoriety for the story of his refusal, as mayor, to allow the Duke of Norfolk's players to enter the city, as a result of which the duke, in pique, had the ancient palace of the dukes of Norfolk demolished. It has always been assumed from this that Havers had puritanical leanings. Perhaps a more likely explanation, recently suggested by Frank Meeres, is that, as a staunch Whig, he and his fellow councillors were worried about possible Jacobite unrest in the city. The duke was the most prominent Catholic in England.

A receipted bill for silver signed by Havers, apparently the only surviving document of its type from an East Anglian silversmith, is now in Norwich Castle Museum & Art Gallery:[5]

> May 25th 1694 Bought of Thomas   }   l s d
> Havers and sold to the Lady Doyly   }   3-0-0
> one silver porringer and one spoon at }
>
> June the 11th 1698 Received of the Lady Dorothy Doyly by the hand of Mr Joseph Walte of Shotesham three pounds in full of this bill I say Received
> > X
> > Tho: Havers

Liquidity was a major problem for seventeenth-century goldsmiths, who often, as here, had to wait years for bills to be paid. It meant that only those with extensive resources, or other business interests, could prosper. Havers also appears in the Gawdy Papers, in a letter dated 1693 addressed to "Oliver Leneve Esq. att Great Witchingham to be left at Mr. havers goldsmith in Norwich".[6]

Thomas Havers married twice, first to Martha (?), who died in 1679, and second to Grace, daughter of Henry Berney of Anmer.[7] The Berneys were considerable landowners in the county. Grace Havers died in 1718 and Thomas died in 1732 aged 86 and was buried in the south chapel of St Michael at Plea, Norwich.[8] The church has an alms basin, struck with Havers' mark but no hallmarks, inscribed *Ex Dono Tho. Havers Eclesiæ Sti. Mich: ad Placita Ano. Dom.*

1694, as well as a pair of flagons made by Havers and with Norwich hallmarks for 1691–2.

1 Thomas Havers the goldsmith and his near-contemporary Thomas Havers of Thelveton Hall had a common great-great-grandfather, John Havers of Winfarthing, who was steward to the Duke of Norfolk: see 1563 Visitation of Norfolk and Burke's *History of the Commoners*, 1865, pp. 381–2.
2 Freemen, Norwich, p. 71.
3 Goldsmiths' Company records 9/172.
4 Barrett, *Norwich Silver*, p. 87.
5 See Barrett, "Document", p. 509.
6 British Library Egerton 2718, vol. VI, f. 40.
7 Norfolk Genealogy vol. 22, *sub* Havers of Swainsthorpe and Norwich.
8 The *Norwich Gazette* for March 3–10, 1732/3 records "Norwich, March 10. On Saturday last past died Thomas Havers, Esq: The Senior Alderman of this City above the Chair, who was Sheriff here in 1701 and Mayor in 1708"; his death is also noted in the *Gentleman's Magazine* for March 10, 1732/3. He appears to have died intestate, perhaps suddenly, and is described in the administration papers as "late of the city of Norwich" (NRO Administration A8 (1733) Norwich Archdeaconry MF377).
9 NA Norwich, p. 98.

34
Trefid spoon *Silver*

Norwich; *c*.1675–1688; maker's mark of Thomas Havers (1646–1732)
Private Collection

With egg-shaped bowl and flat stem, with rat-tail; the reverse of the terminal pricked TF *(or* FT*) conjoined over* BAPT *over July 14 over 1624*

L. 8¼ in. (21 cm)

Marks: Struck on reverse of stem with castle and lion, crown, rose (Jackson, p. 338, line 13) and with maker's mark (Levine, no. 33)

35
Mug *Silver*

Norwich; 1689–90; maker's mark of Thomas Havers (1646–1732)
Private Collection

Circular on spreading foot with slightly flaring sides, flat scroll handle

H. 1½ in. (6.4 cm); W. 3¾ in. (9.5 cm); D. 2⅞ in. (7.5 cm); WEIGHT 2oz. 15 dwt. (85 g)

Marks: Struck under base with castle and lion, crowned rose, date letter lower-case gothic b (Jackson, p. 339, line 2) and with maker's mark (Levine, no. 33)

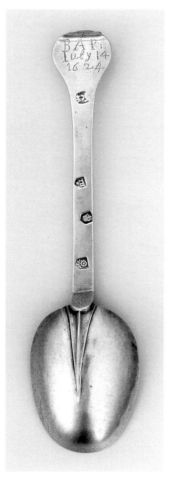

34

35

36

36

Mug *Silver*

Norwich; 1689–90; maker's mark of Thomas Havers
(1646–1732)
Private Collection

Bulbous with straight ribbed neck and reeded strip scroll handle

Mugs of this form are often found in stoneware produced as
early as the 1670s in Fulham by John Dwight and later by
Nottingham potters. Among silver examples a London-
made one of 1688–9 is in the Museum of Fine Arts, Boston.[1]
Several are known from Norwich: a slightly larger example
with Havers' mark and the Norwich town and standard
mark, *c.*1685, is recorded,[2] while the largest of the Norwich
group, some 3⅛ inches high, with the maker's mark ED, is in
the Norwich Castle Museum & Art Gallery.[3] An example of
about 3½ inches high, bearing the mark of Lionel Girling,
who worked in both Norwich and Beccles around 1685, is
also known.[4]

H. 2⅛ in. (5.3 cm); w. 3 in. (7.6 cm); D. 2½ in. (6.4 cm);
WEIGHT 1 OZ. 2 dwt. (37 g)

Marks: Struck under base with castle and lion, crowned rose,
date letter lower-case gothic b (Jackson, p. 339, line 2) and
with maker's mark (Levine, no. 33)

Provenance: Geoffrey Barrett Collection; anonymous sale [G.
Barrett], Christie's, London, March 27, 1985, lot 189, Henry
Levine Ltd., Norwich, from whom purchased by Christine
Winfield in 1986, The Winfield Collection, Bonhams &
Brooks, London, March 6, 2001, lot 192, private collection

1 Alcorn, pp. 178–9, no. 88.
2 Exhibited *Norwich Silver*, Norwich, 1966, no. 100.
3 Emmerson, p. 23, no. 10.
4 Advertised by How of Edinburgh in *Country Life*, January 25, 1979 (I am
   grateful to Miss Hazel Bacon for this reference).

37

Trefid spoon *Silver*

Norwich; 1689–90; maker's mark of Thomas Havers
(1646–1732)
Private Collection

*With egg-shaped bowl and flat stem, with rat-tail; the reverse of
the terminal pricked* B *over* II

This spoon is one of a pair.

L. 7½ in. (9 cm)

Marks: Struck on reverse of stem with castle and lion,
crowned rose, date letter lower-case gothic b (Jackson, p. 339,
line 2) and with maker's mark (Levine, no. 33)

38

37

38

Mug *Silver*

Norwich; 1688–9; maker's mark of Thomas Havers
(1646–1732)
Private Collection

Cylindrical with flaring lip and flat scroll handle, the side pricked
LW *over* 1688

Modest drinking cups of this form have not survived in
great quantities probably because of their light weight and
utilitarian nature. A London example of 1675–6 is in the
Museum of Fine Arts, Boston.[1]

H. 2⅛ in. (5.4 cm); w. 3⅝ in. (9.2 cm); D. 2⅝ in. (6.8 cm);
WEIGHT 2 OZ. 3 dwt. (67 g)

Marks: Struck under base castle and lion, crowned rose, date
letter lower-case gothic a (Jackson, p. 339, line 1) and with-
maker's mark (Levine,
no. 33); the base of the
handle struck with
maker's mark

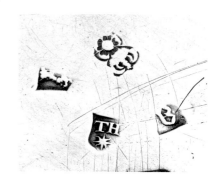

Provenance: Geoffrey Barrett Collection; anonymous sale [G. N. Barrett], Christie's, London, April 27/28, 1983, lot 191; Payne & Son, Oxford, private collection

Published: Norwich Silver, Norwich, p. 35; Barrett, *Norwich Silver,* p. 32

Exhibited: Norwich Silver, Norwich, 1966, no. 104, lent anonymously

1 Alcorn, p. 161, no. 73.

39
Trefid spoon *Silver*

Norwich; *c.*1697–1702; maker's mark of Thomas Havers (1646–1732)
Private Collection

With egg-shaped bowl and flat stem, with rat-tail; the reverse of the terminal pricked IB *over* TM

Growing consumer demand for silver in the prosperous years following the Restoration had, by the 1690s, resulted in a severe shortage of silver coinage in circulation since much if it had been melted down by silversmiths to fill orders for plate. The 1697 Act of Parliament imposed a new higher standard to be used for silverware and by closing all the provincial assay offices concentrated the trade in London. Silversmiths in Norwich responded by striking marks of their own invention on their output; this and the following spoon are among five objects recorded with versions of this "standard" mark.[1] "F SIL" appears to stand for "fine silver" and the initial N for Norwich.

L. 8 in. (20.3 cm)

Marks: Struck on reverse of stem twice with maker's mark (Levine, no. 33) and once with F SIL over an N flanked by a leopard's head and a lion's head erased, all in a rectangular punch (Jackson, p. 339, line 15)

Provenance: How of Edinburgh, The Griffin Collection, sale, Bonhams, London, July 19, 2002, lot 223, private collection

1 The same "standard" mark appears in conjunction with Elizabeth Haslewood's mark on a tankard sold with later chased decoration (Waddington, McLean & Co., Toronto, March 17, 1976, lot 80) and again, without chasing (Christie's, London, June 13, 2001, lot 152), and with James Daniell's mark on two trefid spoons in Norwich Castle Museum & Art Gallery. A spout cup pricked 1701, also in Norwich Castle, has Daniell's mark struck in conjunction with a shield-shaped punch with the figure of Justice above the initial N and an oval punch with F: over SIL (Emmerson, nos. 6, 32 and 33).

40
Trefid spoon *Silver*

Norwich; dated 1697; maker's mark of Thomas Havers (1646–1732)
Private Collection

With egg-shaped bowl and flat stem, with rat-tail; the reverse of the terminal pricked EB *over* TB *over* 1697

L. 7⅛ in. (18 cm)

Marks: Struck on reverse of stem with maker's mark (Levine, no. 33) and with F SIL over an N flanked by a leopard's head and a lion's head erased, all in a rectangular punch (Jackson, p. 339, line 15)

Provenance: Anonymous sale, Sotheby's, London, November 7, 1996, lot 35A, private collection

Published: Barrett, *Norwich Silver,* p. 44

39   40

James Daniell (fl. *c*.1689–after 1715)

(Cat. nos. 41 and 42)

James Daniell appears to have been – along with the Haslewood family and Thomas Havers – the leading producer of plate during the final years of the Norwich assay office. He was admitted free on March 2, 1693[1] as the son of Joseph Daniell without having served an apprenticeship to a Norwich goldsmith. He had been working in Norwich for some time already, however, as his maker's mark appears on objects with earlier date letters, such as the cup, no. 41, and on November 10, 1686 he had been fined £21 by the searchers of the London company of goldsmiths for having in his possession £28 12s 6d worth of substandard gold and silver wares.[2] This was the largest fine incurred and the biggest amount of wares confiscated during that visit. It was a good deal more than that imposed on the Haslewoods and Thomas Havers, perhaps showing the scale of Daniell's business. The reason for the delay in taking up his freedom is explained by the fact that by the end of the seventeenth century, with the guild system in decline, there were probably few business advantages worth the costs involved. Daniell was Sheriff of the city in 1707[3] and is probably the James Daniell who was one of the witnesses to Elizabeth Haslewood's will signed in 1715.[4]

Daniell used two marks: the JD conjoined mark found on the cup, no. 41, and the St Stephen's basin, no. 42, and another, later, mark found after 1696 of JD above a star.[5] This last version of his mark was used by Daniell in conjunction with versions of the pseudo-Britannia marks found on plate made between 1697 and 1702.[6] A flagon belonging to All Saints, Stuston, is struck with a rose mark, ID in a shaped shield and a right hand or glove erect in a shield. These may be marks used by Daniell in the early 1680s.

1 Freemen, Norwich, p. 71.
2 Goldsmiths' Company 9/172v.
3 Levine, p. 301.
4 NRO/NCC Wills/325 Melchior; George Levine read this signature as James Downe.
5 Levine, no. 35.
6 See a spout cup in Norwich Castle Museum & Art Gallery, pricked 1701, illustrated in Emmerson, p. 18.

41

Two-handled cup *Silver*

Norwich; 1691–1; maker's mark of James Daniell (fl. *c*.1689–after 1715)

Private Collection

Of circular form on flat base the lower half chased with spiral gadrooning below a band of punched stylized flowerheads with two part-beaded scroll handles

This two-handled cup, or porringer, is one of two recorded by Daniell, of the same form but with quite different decoration.[1] Both have chased spiral lobing around the lower part and punched leaf decoration above; the same simple punch of a circle has been used on both, but on the later example a flowerhead punch has also been used. The cast handles on the example illustrated here are extremely well defined, with virtually no traces of pitting or bubbling such as that found on the small cup from the Haslewood workshop (no. 23).

H. 3¼ in. (8.2 cm); w. 7 in. (17.8 cm); D. 4⅛ in. (10.4 cm); WEIGHT 6 oz. 12 dwt. (205 g)

Marks: Struck under base with castle and lion, crowned rose, date letter lower-case gothic d (Jackson, p. 339, line 5) and with maker's mark (Levine, no. 34)

Provenance: Walter H. Willson Ltd., 1938; Geoffrey Barrett Collection; anonymous sale [G. N. Barrett], Christie's, London, March 27, 1985, lot 193 (unsold), anonymous sale, Christie's, New York, October 15, 1985, lot 195; Keith Heathcote, Badlingham Manor, Chippenham, Cambridgeshire, house sale, Vost's, September 16, 1999, private collection

Published: The Connoisseur, November 1938, p. 64; *Norwich Silver*, Norwich, p. 33; Barrett, *Norwich Silver*, illus. p. 76 and on the back cover

Exhibited: Norwich Silver, Norwich, 1966, no. 111, lent anonymously

1 The other, with the 1696–7 date letter, with flat reeded handles, is in Norwich Castle Museum & Art Gallery (Emmerson, p. 17).

41

42

42

Alms basin *Silver*

Norwich; 1691–2; maker's mark of James Daniell
(fl. *c.*1689–after 1715)
St Stephen's Church, Norwich

Of deep circular form with flat reeded rim; engraved underneath
Given to St Stephen's Church Norwich Ano Dom 1694 *and
around the rim (probably in the eighteenth century)* He that
gives to the Poor Lends to the Lord

H. 1¾ in. (4.5 cm); DIAM. 9½ in. (24 cm)

Marks: Struck on rim with castle and lion, crowned rose,
date letter lower-case gothic d (Jackson. p. 339, line 5) and
with maker's mark ID conjoined in a shaped punch (Levine,
no. 34)

Published: NA Norwich, p. 110; Jackson, p. 339, line 5 (marks
from this piece illustrated)

43

Small trefid spoon *Silver*

Norwich; *c.*1695; unidentified maker
The Ticktum Collection

With egg shaped bowl, the front of the notched terminal pricked
E *over* AP

This trefid is one of the earliest examples of a spoon of
"dessert spoon" size and is possibly unique in Norwich silver.

L. 6½ in. (16.5 cm)

Marks: Struck on stem with castle and lion and crowned rose
(Jackson, p. 337, line 4); other marks worn

43

The "leopard's head and fleur-de-lis" group
(c.1649–c.1683)
(Cat. nos. 44–61)

One of the most perplexing aspects of seventeenth-century East Anglian silver is the presence of a large group of pieces struck with pseudo-hallmarks and a mark formed of the letters TS, or ST, conjoined.[1] The group can be ascribed to East Anglia, and more specifically to Norfolk, by the presence of six pieces of plate struck with these marks remaining in churches to the south-west and north-east of Norwich.

In addition to these six church pieces, the group includes a further seventeen domestic objects so far recorded, and it is hoped that more may come to light. With five exceptions,[2] all of the group is included in this exhibition. This has enabled the punches used to be studied and also for the TS/ST mark to be compared with the maker's mark of Timothy Skottowe, a Norwich maker who has, over the years, been credited with making most of these objects. However, the style of the two-handled cups and tankards in the group is definitely post-Restoration, while three of the spoons are trefids, a type of spoon that first appeared in the mid-1660s. Moreover, evidently contemporary dates pricked on thirteen out of the twenty-three pieces range between 1649 and 1683. And Skottowe died in 1645.

A spread in dates of some thirty-four years is puzzling: for while a worker *might* have had such a long career, it is nonetheless unusual in the seventeenth century, and the punches may have been used by more than one generation of craftsmen.

Geoffrey Barrett, writing in 1986, suggested Norwich as the location of the workshop on account of the fact that the recorded church pieces are in villages that neatly ring the city at a maximum distance of seventeen miles. It is evident from the quality of the group, and its size, that it emanated from a large and successful workshop. It would have had more than one journeyman, and one or more apprentices. This excludes any other town in the vicinity of Norwich. But why a Norwich craftsman – and a very competent one – should continue to mark his wares with punches clearly in imitation of London hallmarks and have escaped disciplinary action by the London goldsmiths' company is baffling. The reason is probably because by the late 1640s the effects of the long Civil War were being felt even in

Norwich, which had escaped the fighting even though the cathedral had been stripped and the bishop dispossessed. Trade continued but no visits by the London company's wardens took place in Norwich between 1635 and 1686. The Norwich goldsmiths' guild had presumably also fallen on hard times.

The hallmark cycle established in 1624–5 seems to have been last used in 1642 with the date letter T. In that year Timothy Skottowe served for the last time as joint warden of the goldsmiths' company and accepted, perhaps reluctantly, an entirely different post, that of Receiver of Plate, charged with melting down the thousands of silver articles being collected as loans at eight per cent interest to aid the Parliamentary cause. From the mid 1640s onwards silversmiths appear to have struck their own marks on their wares, usually variations, often crude, of the old castle and lion town mark, the rose, and the crown. The maker's mark of William Haydon appears with one version of these marks on beakers dating from about 1645 and Arthur Haslewood I's mark appears with other versions of the same marks on spoons dated through the 1650s. After the Restoration, more silversmiths' marks appear in conjunction with these "pseudo-Norwich" marks, reflecting the growth in trade after 1660, but there is such as broad range of styles and punch outlines that it seems likely that they were workshop marks rather than official assay punches. These would not be re-established until 1688.

Do we have, therefore, an unidentified maker working in Norwich during the Commonwealth and Restoration period using punches that are completely unrelated to those used by the Haslewoods and others? The marks on all of the pieces of this group that are included in this catalogue, with the exception of no. 44, have been compared using high magnification and it appears that the same punches were used thoughout the period.

The marks in question comprise a boldly drawn feline head, obviously inspired by the London town mark of a

Fig. 25 (*right*) Marks from the beaker no. 44

Fig. 26 (*far right*) Marks from the two-handled cup, no. 58

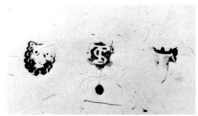
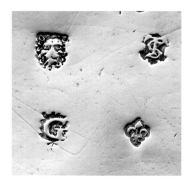

leopard's head but without the crown, the TS/ST conjoined mark, a fleur-de-lis, and, with one exception, a capital roman G in a contoured punch with a distinctive small trefoil below. However, there is one piece, a beaker (no. 44), with proportions and engraved decoration of the middle years of the century, that furnishes us with a link with Norwich and the second date letter cycle. Like the others it bears the TS/ST mark, but rather than a G it has an upper-case roman T with pronounced serifs in a shaped punch that is virtually indistinguishable from the official Norwich date letter of 1642–3. As for the TS/ST mark, it is much akin to Timothy Skottowe's own mark. It could be that the workshop that used this mysterious group of marks had taken over Skottowe's business and cut punches in imitation of his maker's mark, although that is hard to reconcile with the fact that the last apprentice of Skottowe to be made free had been William Skerry as far back as 1627.

One possible candidate as the user of these marks is Edward Wright, who was admitted free on June 28, 1649.[3] Wright was the son of the Edward Wright who had served as assay master for seven annual terms between 1624 and 1635. It is clear that the family were prominent in the trade in the city and did business with the Low Countries[4] but no mark has been identified for them,[5] The year Wright the younger was made free was also that of the execution of Charles I and trade had not fully recovered, so perhaps it is not surprising that the two earliest dated pieces bearing these marks are simple spoons engraved 1649; a gap ensues until the early 1660s when we encounter the marks on a succession of extremely well-made objects such as the flagon (no. 46), reflecting the boom in trade following the Restoration.

The significance of the marks used in the group is interesting. The leopard's head and fleur-de-lis both appeared on the Alnager's seal used in Norfolk and Suffolk. The feline head is clearly inspired by London marks. The fleur-de-lis in various forms is found in a number of locations in England (for a discussion of its use in Bury St Edmunds see p. 109) but it seems to have been most used in East Anglia. It was a familiar symbol, appearing prominently in the first and fourth quarter of both the first and fourth grand quarter of the royal arms of both the Tudors and Stuarts. In addition, fleurs-de-lis appeared on many of the coins in circulation, not only on English but also on French coins which circulated widely and were traditionally seen as being more reliable than the debased and often "clipped" English coins. It is easy to see how the fleur-de-lis could be used as a "symbol of quality". The use of the letter G is more puzzling; the letter is found on Ipswich-made plate of the sixteenth century (see no. 93) and it was to be used by the Hutchinson

family of Great Yarmouth in the 1680s and 90s (see nos. 79–81) but any meaning it may have had in Norfolk, except to suggest an official date letter perhaps, is obscure.[6] The conjoined initials TS or ST are perhaps best seen as signifying sterling standard; in this context they were also used by Wiliam Howlett of King's Lynn (with the S reversed) [see no. 88] and in other locations.

Certain characteristics distinguish the "leopard's head and fleur-de-lis" group. The quality is unvaryingly good with a high degree of finish. Components such as foot rims are extremely well defined and edges are almost razor sharp; the foot rims of the tankard (no. 61) and the beakers (no. 59) should be compared with the foot rims typically found on pieces from the Haslewood or Havers workshops (for example, nos. 21, 22 and 35) with their much less well-defined bolection moulding. Overall, the pieces in the group have a compactness of scale and degree of finish that suggests great skill but little contact, by way of exchange of components or resources, with the other leading workshops of the city.

1 I am grateful to Timothy Kent, Timothy Schroder and Wynyard Wilkinson for illuminating discussions concerning these marks; Timothy Schroder generously gave me his catalogue entry for the beaker (no. 44) from his forthcoming catalogue of the silver in the Ashmolean Museum, Oxford.

2 They are a seal-top spoon dated 1650, formerly in the Ellis Collection, sold Sotheby's, London, November 13–14, 1935, lot 79; an engraved beaker, dated 1678, sold Christie's, London, March 17, 1987, lot 369; a trefid spoon dated 1673 sold Phillips, London, June 18, 1982, lot 139B; a tankard similar to no. 61 sold Sotheby's, New York, December 13, 1984, lot 171; and a trefid spoon described as struck with the fleur-de-lis, the ST conjoined and "two other marks", sold Sotheby's, London, May 2 1963, lot 74.

3 Freemen, Norwich, p. 70.

4 Barrett, *Norwich Silver*, 1981, p. 96.

5 Barrett suggested that Wright the younger may have succeeded his father as assay master during the Commonwealth, as he had as an apprentice Robert Harsonge (free in 1672), who is the only other recorded Norwich assay master, appointed in 1702 (ibid., p. 96) but the lack of consistency of surviving Norwich marks during the Commonwealth and Restoration period may indicate that no assay master was in office.

6 A crowned G was used as a verification mark for wool weights. One such weight at Newby Hall, Yorkshire has the Stuart arms on it.

44

Marks: Struck on rim with feline mask, ST in monogram, T in shaped shield and fleur-de-lis (Jackson, p. 347, line 3) (fig. 25)

Provenance: Mr Samuel of Norwich (dealer)[1]; William Minet, FSA; the Ashmolean Museum, Oxford, presented by Miss Susan Minet, 1949, WA1949.179

Published: W. Minet (1889), pp. 451–2, pls. III and VI; *Park Lane*, London, cat. no. 318, pl. III; *Ashmolean Museum: Annual Report*, 1949, p. 39; Skottowe, illustrated plate facing p. 76 (as by Timothy Skottowe)

Exhibited: Park Lane, London, 1929, no. 318

1 Benjamin Samuel, watchmaker, jeweller, clothier, pawnbroker, and dealer in curiosities and works of art, is listed in Hamilton's *Directory of Norwich*, 1879, at 2–5 Timberhill; he appears in subsequent directories until 1904.

45

Seal-top spoon *Silver*

Norfolk, probably Norwich; dated 1649; unidentified maker
Usher Art Gallery, Lincoln

With fig-shaped bowl, with tapering flat hexagonal stem and fluted baluster knop; the top engraved with the initials AB over 1649 over GB

Another seal-top spoon with similar marks, dated 1650, is recorded.[1]

L. 6⅝ in. (16.8 cm)

Marks: Struck in bowl with feline mask, the back of the stem struck with ST in monogram near the bowl and with fleur-de-lis at the top (Jackson, p. 347, line 6)

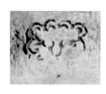

44

Beaker *Silver*

Norfolk, probably Norwich; mid seventeenth century; unidentified maker
The Ashmolean Museum, Oxford (not exhibited)

Tapering cylindrical with slightly everted lip and on spreading foot with an applied ring above; the upper part engraved with horizontal strapwork cartouches enclosing foliage and with three panels of scrolling foliage

H. 5⅝ in. (14.3 cm); DIAM. 3¼ in. (8.3 cm);
WEIGHT 6 oz. 5 dwt. (195 g)

45

Provenance: Viscount Crookshank of Gainsborough, Usher Art Gallery, Lincoln, acquired in 1961 (UG 2478)

1 Formerly in the H. D. Ellis Collection, then by descent to Lieutenant-Colonel J. Benett-Stanford, Pythouse, Tisbury, Wiltshire, sale, Sotheby's, London, November 13–14, 1935, lot 79 (bt. Martin).

46

Flagon *Silver*

Norfolk, probably Norwich; dated 1664; unidentified maker
St Margaret's Church, Paston, Norfolk

The slightly tapering cylindrical body on spreading foot, with moulded rim and tubular scroll handle; the hinged domed cover with plain reeded thumb-piece; the front pricked:
A COMUNION*FLAGON+FOR+THE+TOUN+OF PASTON / GIVEN ANO DNI 1664

H. 10 in. (25.5 cm); W. 9 in. (23 cm); D. 6¼ in. (15.8 cm)

Marks: Struck on side of bowl with feline mask, ST in monogram, G and fleur-de-lis (Jackson, p. 347, line 6)

Published: Barrett, "Problem Solved", p. 313

47

Cup and paten *Silver*

Norfolk, probably Norwich; dated 1664; unidentified maker
St Botolph's Church, Morley, Norfolk

The cylindrical bowl with slightly flaring lip, on cast baluster stem and spreading circular foot; the bowl engraved + FOR THE TOVN OF MORLE BVTELS + 1664 +

This cup, a secular goblet, is virtually identical with the cup of Carleton Forehoe (no. 48) and the smaller one at Horsey (no. 49) from the same workshop. All are made using the same techniques and have an unusually large strengthening flange under the bowl. It is unusual to find engraving on work from this workshop (see no. 51); from the style of the inscription, and the spelling, it is evident that this cup replaced an Elizabethan example in 1664 and the original inscription copied. The paten has no marks and it is impossible to say if it was supplied with the cup; the engraved *Morley* on the reverse is in the style of the second half of the seventeenth century.

H. 5⅝ in. (14.3 cm); DIAM. 3½ in. (9 cm)

Marks: Struck on side of bowl with feline mask, ST in monogram, G and fleur-de-lis (Jackson, p. 347, line 6)

Published: Barrett, "Problem Solved", p. 313

46

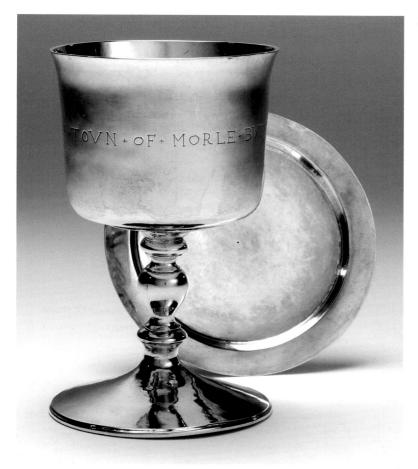

47

48

48

Cup *Silver*

Norfolk, probably Norwich; *c.*1665–1675; unidentified maker

St Mary's Church, Carleton Forehoe, Norfolk

The cylindrical bowl with slightly flaring lip, on cast baluster stem and spreading circular foot; the bowl pricked with the initials CF *within an oval cartouche of scrolls*

Secular cups of this form are usually described as "beer bowls" in contemporary inventories. The pricked initials and cartouche on the side are in the style used for domestic silver; here the initals CF evidently stand for Carleton Forehoe. It is not known when the cup was acquired by Carleton Forehoe for use as a communion cup.

H. 5⅝ in. (14.3 cm); DIAM. 3½ in. (9 cm)

Marks: Struck on side of bowl with feline mask, ST in monogram, G and fleur-de-lis (Jackson, p. 347, line 6)

Published: Barrett, "Problem Solved", p. 313

49

Cup *Silver*

Norfolk, probably Norwich; dated 1666; unidentified maker
All Saints Church, Horsey, Norfolk

The cylindrical bowl with slightly flaring lip, on cast baluster stem and spreading circular foot; the bowl inscribed For the Towne of Horfsee in the County of Norfolk Ano Dom. 1666 *and below* HP WM

H. 4½ in. (11.4 cm); DIAM. 2½ in. (6.4 cm); WEIGHT 3 OZ. (93 g)

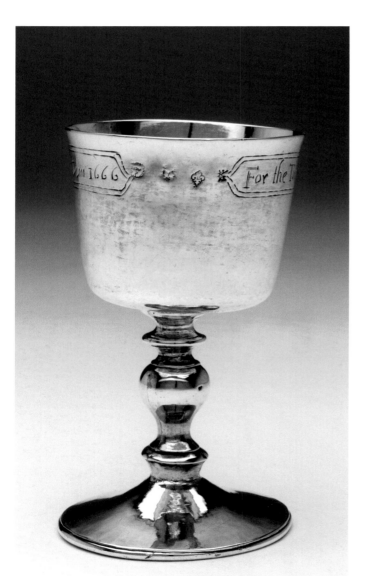

49

Marks: Struck on side of bowl with feline mask, ST in monogram, G and fleur-de-lis (Jackson, p. 347, line 6)

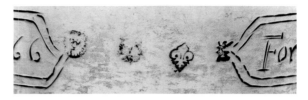

Published: Barrett, "Problem Solved", p. 313

50

Paten *Silver*

Norfolk, probably Norwich; *c.*1660–80; unidentified maker
All Saints Church, Shipdham, Norfolk

Plain circular with broad flat rim

DIAM. 9 in. (22.8 cm)

Marks: Struck on rim with feline mask, ST in monogram, G and fleur-de-lis (Jackson, p. 347, line 6)

Published: Barrett, "Problem Solved", p. 313

51

Paten *Silver*

Norfolk, probably Norwich; dated 1674; unidentified maker
St Margaret's Church, Hardwick, Norfolk

Plain circular with broad flat rim, raised on a plain spool foot; the rim engraved Donum Petri Gleane Baronetti Ecclesiæ Parochiali Hardwici Anno 1674

Peter Gleane of Hardwick succeeded his father, Thomas Gleane, in 1660 and was created a baronet by Charles II. He married Penelope, daughter and co-heiress of Edward Rodney, but he was unable to stop the slow decline of the family's fortunes. His heavily mortgaged estates were acquired by Sir John Holland shortly after his death in 1694. Sir Peter Gleane and his wife are buried under the altar of St Margaret's Church.[1]

50

51

H. 2 in. (5 cm); DIAM. 8¾ in (22.4 cm)

Marks: Struck on rim with feline mask, ST in monogram, G and fleur-de-lis (Jackson, p. 347, line 6)

Published: Barrett, "Problem Solved", p. 313

1 *History and Antiquities of the County of Norfolk*, Norwich, 1781, vol. 2, p. 106.

52
Trefid spoon *Silver*

Norfolk, probably Norwich; dated 1674; unidentified maker
The Ticktum Collection

With egg-shaped bowl and flat stem, with rat-tail; the reverse of the terminal pricked RT *over* WB *over* 74

L. 8 in. (20.4 cm)

Marks: Struck on reverse of stem with feline mask, ST in monogram, G and fleur-de-lis (Jackson, p. 347, line 6)

Provenance: H. D. Ellis Collection, Lieutenant-Colonel J. Benett-Stanford, Pythouse, Tisbury, Wiltshire, sale, Sotheby's, London, November 13–14, 1935, lot 77 (bt. How of Edinburgh Ltd.); the Griffin Collection; the Ticktum Collection

53
Trefid spoon *Silver*

Norfolk, probably Norwich; dated 1683; unidentified maker
Private Collection

With egg-shaped bowl and flat stem, with rat-tail; the reverse of the terminal pricked F *over* TM *over* 1683

L. 7½ in. (19 cm)

Marks: Struck on reverse of stem with feline mask, ST in monogram, G and fleur-de-lis (Jackson, p. 347, line 6)

Provenance: H. D. Ellis Collection, Lieutenant-Colonel J. Benett-Stanford, Pythouse, Tisbury, Wiltshire, sale, Sotheby's, London, November 13–14, 1935, lot 78, private collection

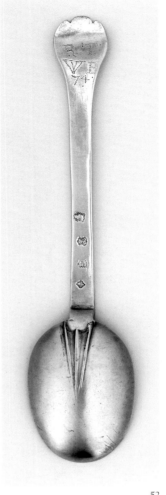
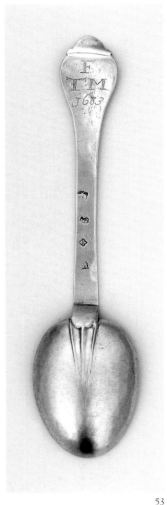

52   53

54

54

Beaker *Silver*

Norfolk, probably Norwich; *c.*1649–1683; unidentified maker

Usher Art Gallery, Lincoln

Of slightly flaring straight-sided form on moulded base, the sides engraved with three large fleurs-de-lis under a horizontal band of compartments enclosing foliate sprays

H. 3¹⁄₈ in. (7.9 cm); DIAM. 3 in. (7.25 cm)

Marks: Struck under base with feline mask, ST in monogram, G and fleur-de-lis (Jackson, p. 347, line 6)

Provenance: Viscount Crookshank of Gainsborough, Usher Art Gallery, Lincoln, acquired in 1961 (UG 2477)

Published: Skottowe, illustrated opposite p. 12 (as by Timothy Skottowe)

55

55

Beaker *Silver*

Norfolk, probably Norwich; *c.*1649–1683; unidentified maker

Usher Art Gallery, Lincoln

Of slightly flaring straight-sided form on moulded base, the sides engraved with criss-crossing foliate sprigs and scrolls under a ruled horizontal band; the side engraved with the initials ?JJH

H. 3⁵⁄₈ in. (9.7 cm); DIAM. 3³⁄₈ in. (8.2 cm)

Marks: Struck under base with feline mask, ST in monogram, G and fleur-de-lis (Jackson, p. 347, line 6)

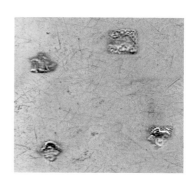

Provenance: Viscount Crookshank of Gainsborough, Usher Art Gallery, Lincoln, acquired in 1961 (UG 2476)

56

57

Two-handled cup *Silver*

Norfolk, probably Norwich; dated 1678; unidentified maker
Private Collection

Of circular form on flat base with slightly flaring sides, with two plain reeded scroll handles; the side pricked with the initials AY *over* FY *over the date* 1678

H. 2¼ in. (5.6 cm); w. 4¾ in. (12 cm); D. 2¾ in. (7 cm);
WEIGHT I OZ. 19 dwt. (60 g)

Marks: Struck under base with feline mask, ST in monogram, G and fleur-de-lis (Jackson, p. 347, line 6); also with ?workman's mark of an engraved cross close to the centring mark under the base

Provenance: Anonymous sale, Sotheby's, London, May 29, 1975, lot 139; private collection

58

Two-handled cup *Silver*

Norfolk, probably Norwich; *c.*1660–1683; unidentified maker
Private Collection

Of circular baluster form on flat base, with two scroll handles; engraved under the base with the initials SR *and later with the date* Aug 1st 1725

H. 3 in. (7.6 cm); w. 6½ in. (16.5 cm); D. 4½ in. (11.5 cm);
WEIGHT 5 OZ. 8 dwt. (168 g)

Marks: Struck under base with feline mask, ST in monogram, G and fleur-de-lis (Jackson, p. 347, line 6)

Provenance: Anonymous sale, Phillips, London, May 4, 1968 (bt. Swonnell); private collection

56

Beaker *Silver*

Norfolk, probably Norwich; *c.*1649–1683; unidentified maker
Usher Art Gallery, Lincoln

Of slightly flaring straight-sided form on moulded base the sides engraved with large foliate scrolls with pendent stylized thistles and, under the rim, with a band of foliage in interlacing cartouches, side engraved with the initials EB *over* SB

H. 3¾ in. (9.8 cm); DIAM. 3¼ in. (7.9 cm)

Marks: Struck under base with feline mask, ST in monogram, G and fleur-de-lis (Jackson, p. 347, line 6)

Provenance: Viscount Crookshank of Gainsborough, Usher Art Gallery, Lincoln, acquired in 1961 (UG 2475)

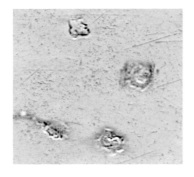

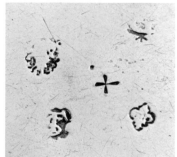

57 (marks)   57

58

59

59

Pair of beakers *Silver*

Norfolk, probably Norwich; *c.*1649–1683; unidentified maker

Private Collection

Of slightly flaring straight-sided form on moulded bases with flat flanges; the sides engraved (probably in the nineteenth century) with a crest of a pelican vulning herself in a basket

H. 3¼ in. (8.2 cm); DIAM. 2⅝ in. (6.7 cm); WEIGHT 3 oz. 4 dwt. (99 g)

Marks: Struck under rims with feline mask, ST in monogram, G and fleur-de-lis (Jackson, p. 347, line 6)

Provenance: How of Edinburgh Ltd.

60

Spout cup *Silver*

Norfolk, probably Norwich; *c.*1649–1683; unidentified maker

The Museum of Fine Arts, Boston

Baluster on plain flat base with straight-sided foot; the narrowing neck with wide straight rim incised with four lines; the hinged slightly domed cover with lion's mask thumb-piece; the strap scroll handle with serrated terminal; with scroll tubular handle at right angles; the top of the handle engraved DD

Comparatively few spouted tankards and porringers have survived from the seventeenth century, although wills and inventories, which usually refer to them as "posset pots", show them to have been relatively common. A possible explanation is that the slender spout was always prone to damage, but perhaps more likely is the reason given by Commander How, who remarked in the 1940s how silver dealers of the previous generation had removed hundreds of spouts from these items in order to make more saleable plain porringers and "ladies'" tankards. Posset was a hot drink of curdled milk or cream combined with sack (sherry) or ale, spices and sugar. Gervaise Markham, in his book *The English Housewife* (1615), gives a recipe for posset as a preventative for colds. It was often taken in bed at the end of the day. The tube enabled one to drink the liquor and avoid the foam on top. Several East Anglian spout cups survive, including one

60

by Timothy Skottowe of Norwich (no. 13) and one by James Daniell of about 1700 in Norwich Castle Museum & Art Gallery. The form of this pot, with its broad vertical rim, follow pewter measures of the period, but this is a virtually unique example in silver.

H. 4¾ in. (12 cm); W. 4⁵⁄₁₆ in. (11 cm); D. 3¹³⁄₁₆ in. (9.7 cm); WEIGHT 8 oz. 11 dwt. (269 g)

Marks: Struck on cover with feline mask, ST in monogram, G and fleur-de-lis (Jackson, p. 347, line 6)

Provenance: G. J. Levine, Norwich; J. H. Barnes, sale, Christie's London, November 29, 1961, lot 117 (bt. Thomas Lumley), Museum of Fine Arts, Boston, Theodora Wilbour Fund in Memory of Charlotte Beebe Wilbour, acquired in 1962 (62.672)

Published: Holland, p. 113, illustrated p. 103; Glanville, *Tudor and Early Stuart*, p. 438; Alcorn, pp. 124–5, no. 51

61

61

Tankard *Silver*

Norfolk, probably Norwich; *c*.1660–1680; unidentified maker

Private Collection

Of slightly tapering cylindrical; form on moulded foot, with tubular scroll handle and bifurcated thumb-piece and flat hinged cover; the top of the handle pricked with the initials K *over* AM *within scrolls; pricked under the base* IY ?an *and* iii ?.

Another tankard with the same marks is recorded, pricked with the date 1678.[1]

H. 5¼ in. (13.3 cm); W. 6¾ in. (17 cm); D. 4½ in. (11.4 cm); WEIGHT 16 oz. 18 dwt. (525 g)

Marks: Struck under base with feline mask, ST in monogram, G and fleur-de-lis (Jackson, p. 347, line 6)

Provenance: Anonymous sale, Sotheby's, London, February 27, 1981, lot 123; private collection

1 The tankard, of identical form to the present example, measuring 5⅝ in.(14.3 cm) high was sold by Sotheby's, New York, February 27, 1981, lot 123.

Decorated spoons of Norfolk and Suffolk

Decoration on seventeenth-century East Anglian spoons

Timothy Kent

It is becoming clear that certain decorative features of locally made spoons are uniquely East Anglian. While the process of discovery continues, this exhibition will do much to identify decorative themes in this important group. For, apart from the interesting York Group, the two main areas of English spoon making outside London were undoubtedly the West Country and East Anglia. The reason is not hard to find: these were areas of substantial prosperity, where clothiers, farmers, and mercantile entrepreneurs had spare cash in their pockets to spend on the luxuries of life.

It might be supposed that London-made spoons would show a higher degree of quality and sophistication than country spoons, and indeed the goldsmiths outside London never produced, or were required to produce, anything like the famous Tichborne Celebrities (William Cawdell, 1592–3). However some provincial examples, such as the engraved Barnstaple spoons ascribed to the Quick family workshop, c.1620, have a character and fascination which London-made spoons cannot match. The decoration of this group, and indeed the "Aphrodites" and "Buddhas" from the same area, show strong Continental influence, which is hardly surprising when one reflects on the importance and prosperity of Barnstaple as a trading port.

When we come to East Anglian ports this point is highly relevant. For example, no. 86 has a distinctive stem not encountered elsewhere on English spoons, and were it not for the form of the bowl, the way in which the bowl and lower stem are made from one piece, and the presence of the maker's mark of James Wilcocke of King's Lynn on it, one would think it to be Dutch. Links with towns in the Low Countries were extremely strong in King's Lynn and the port supported a large community of Dutch and Flemish traders. It is tempting to think that this spoon was commissioned by a local merchant to extend an existing set of Continental examples.

Local spoon makers were not slow to develop their own particular decorative styles. In the West Country, Salisbury seal-top castings of the 1620–1650 period are unmistakable, and probably emanate from one specialist workshop in that city. In the period from 1660 to 1680 the formalized scratch-engraving to be found on Barnstaple puritan spoons from the Peard family workshop appears to be confined almost exclusively to that borough, just as engraved rat-tails on trefids of the 1680–1700 period seem to be confined to Exeter and Tiverton spoons. Taunton seal-castings, too, are distinctive. Many lace-back trefids (1675–1700) are readily assigned to particular areas by reason of highly individualistic dies, sometimes pertaining to families or dynasties, such as the Dares of Taunton, the Servants of Barnstaple and Bideford, or the widespread Sweet Family of Crewkerne, Chard, Dunster and Honiton. Another fascinating group is that which features "shaded roundel" stem decoration on trefid spoons of the 1670–1680 period, formerly given a tentative ascription to Cornwall but now placed firmly in mid-Wessex by a "link" spoon with the unequivocal maker's mark of Oliver Arden of Sherborne (d. 1684). The presence of "link spoons" in the East Anglian context is similarly crucial.

Over the past two decades, research in the West Country has brought a great deal of new information to light, mainly by a detailed examination of church plate and investigation of the Court Minute Books of the London goldsmiths' company, with their record of searches in the area.[1] While a certain amount has been done for East Anglia, for example in the catalogue of the exhibition *Lynn Silver* prepared by the Rev. James Gilchrist and Brand Inglis for an exhibition in 1972, and the researches of Geoffrey Barrett and George Levine, much remains to be done, particularly for south Norfolk and the county of Suffolk. Church plate needs to be viewed systematically and marks photographed. The bringing together of objects for this exhibition allows some observations to be made: for example the distinctive die used for lace-back trefids by the Hutchinson workshop of Great Yarmouth (nos. 80 and 81) in the 1680s.

Reference to the importance of "link" spoons has already been made. Item no. 62, a fully marked Norwich seal-top of 1631–2 with the maker's mark of Timothy Skottowe, is one of a small group of Norwich-marked spoons which firmly anchors the distinctive engraved decoration on the bowl within the East Anglian catchment area.[2] The simple arabesques, lozenges, and trapezoidal reservation for initials, contained within a zigzag border which is similar to the distinctive assay gouge found on Norwich silver, are constant features of this group. The eight spoons which follow in this catalogue (nos. 62–9), of which seven appear to retain their original gilding, form a representative selection of this East Anglian school of spoon decoration.

The attractive spoon, item no. 67, with bowl decoration falling positively within this group, has a maker's mark RD struck in its bowl and an engraved date 1601, and for reasons given on p. 90 an ascription to Robert Dale II of Woodbridge (d. 1614) is reasonable. It has engraved initials on the cap, and although no absolute rule can be laid down, engraving rather than pricking seems to have been more common in East Anglia than elsewhere.

Similar decoration is found on a number of seal tops with device, rather than initial, marks. In some cases an East Anglian provenance, or the presence of the same or similar marks on church plate in the region, provide us with the link. A seal top belonging to St Peter Parmentergate in Norwich (no. 63), which has had a cross added to the seal, is of this decorative group; the decoration incorporates the initials EW and date 1613. When the spoon was acquired by the church is not known, but, writing about this spoon in the 1860s, the Rev. C. R. Manning cited the suggestion of the then rector of the parish that the spoon had been the christening spoon of Edward Warnes, the benefactor of a valuable estate to the parish on his death in 1700. The spoon is struck in the bowl with a stylized fleur-de-lis, or trefoil, in a serrated circle; a similar mark appears on church plate in Suffolk and on other spoons with East Anglian bowl decoration such as no. 64, dated 1608. Item nos. 65 and 66 also have a trefoil bowl mark, and, although dated 1600 and 1609, bear seal-cap engraving by the same hand or workshop and clearly come from the same stable. The engraver, perhaps coached by the local parson, got his Latin genders right, *natus* for a boy, *nata* for a girl respectively. A definite East Anglian feel, but in any event these two fine spoons show the hand of a master craftsman.

Other spoons noted with the distinctively East Anglian engraved decoration on the back of the bowl include a seal top dated 1606, formerly in the Ellis Collection[3] and another sold at Phillips in 1982.[4] The Ellis example is struck with a variation of the pelleted mark of the Waveney Valley; as Commander How noted in the catalogue, the identical punch is found on communion cups at Barnby and Gislingham. The Phillips example is dated 1596 and is struck with an undoubted East Anglian quatrefoil mark. Another example, no. 68, though evidently within the decorative group, is more lavish in its application and may be of a somewhat later date than the others. Its pelleted bowl mark is also found on church plate in the Beccles area, but a much more detailed survey of the variations of these pellet marks is necessary.

Variations of the East Anglian engraved bowl decoration appear front and back on no. 69, the magnificent seal-top formerly in the G. S. Sanders Collection. In Sanders' MS catalogue[5] it was ascribed to Raleigh Clapham of Barnstaple, oddly as the spoon is pricked 1622 and Clapham was born in 1629. The decoration on this spoon is lavish but clearly falls into the East Anglia group and an ascription to Richard Chesten of Beccles seems sensible. Documentary evidence dating from 1915 to 1919 and emanating from the Diss area, which described another spoon with the same bowl mark as "the old family spoon", provides cogent support for a Norfolk-Suffolk border origin. A spoon of this impressive size would have been a commission of importance, and it would be fascinating to discover a local yeoman or merchant who used a horse or donkey as his badge.[6]

1 Kent, *West Country Silver Spoons*, pp. 33–46.
2 The J. H. Walter sale (July 1–2, 1954) included two additional seal tops with similar decoration, both by Arthur Haslewood I of Norwich (lots 152 and 155). Lot 152 passed into the collection of G. S. Sanders and a drawing in his MS catalogue (S74) shows clearly the decoration in question.
3 H. D. Ellis Collection, Lieutenant-Colonel J. Benett-Stanford, Pythouse, Tisbury, Wiltshire, sale, Sotheby's, London, November 13–14, 1935, lot 242.
4 June 18, 1982, lot 194.
5 S75.
6 Papworth's *Ordinary of Armorials* lists no Norfolk or Suffolk family with an equine heraldic charge but it may well be a case of an assumed device rather than an official grant or confirmation of arms.

62

62

Seal-top spoon[1] *Silver, parcel-gilt*

Norwich, 1631–2; maker's mark of Timothy Skottowe
(fl. 1617–1645)
Private Collection

*With fig-shaped bowl and hexagonal stem with baluster seal, the
lower portion with boldly scratch engraved decoration; engraved
on back of bowl with a vacant trapezoidal cartouche with scrolls,
lozenges and simple arabesques at intervals all within a zigzag
border; pricked on seal LR over MA and with date 1632*

Two other Norwich seal-top spoons with similar engraved
decoration are recorded, one with the maker's mark of
Arthur Haslewood I.[2]

L. 6¾ in. (17.1 cm)

Marks: struck in bowl with crowned rose, and on reverse of
stem with castle and lion, date letter upper-case roman H
and with maker's mark TS conjoined, possibly overstriking
another (Jackson, p. 337, line 8[3]); a further crowned rose
struck over the lap joint under the terminal[4]

Provenance: Purchased from a private source by Messrs
Croydon, Ipswich, *c*.1960; Geoffrey Barrett Collection,
anonymous sale [G. Barrett] Christie's London April 27/28,
1983, lot 182, private collection

Published: Clayton, *History*, p. 60, no. 1

1 This catalogue entry was prepared in collaboration with Timothy Kent.
2 See p. 86, note 2.
3 Taken from this spoon.
4 Commander How, when discussing the only recorded Norwich spoon
   with Virgin and Child terminal (1635-6, maker's mark a lion rampant,
   now in Norwich Castle Museum & Art Gallery), remarks that "it will be
   seen that the Rose Crowned, struck in the bowl, has also been struck at
   the top of the stem across the join where the finial is applied, proving
   conclusively that the finial is original. This valuable practice of striking a
   mark at the junction of finial and stem would appear to have been
   customary in Norwich at this period, but I have not noted it on English
   spoons made elsewhere." (How, *Spoons*, vol. 2, p. 168).

63

Seal-top spoon[1] *Silver*

East Anglia, probably Suffolk; dated 1613; unidentified maker

St Peter Parmentergate Church, Norwich

With fig-shaped bowl and with slightly hexagonal stem and fluted baluster finial; the top later applied with a roughly cast crucifix; the back of the bowl engraved with East Anglian decoration featuring a fleur-de-lis and a trapezoidal reservation enclosing the initials EW and date 1613, with a zigzag border

The mark is identical to that struck on the spoon no. 64. Both spoons are clearly from the same workshop as the baluster seal terminals are from the same mould. A similar mark appears on a communion cup dated 1586 belonging to All Saints Church, Debach, Suffolk.[2]

L. 7⅜ in. (18.8 cm)

Mark: struck in bowl with a stylized fleur-de-lis or trefoil in beaded circular punch

Published: NA, Norwich, p. 106

1 This catalogue entry was prepared in collaboration with Timothy Kent.
2 SCP Loes, *sub* Debach.

64

Seal-top spoon[1] *Silver, parcel-gilt*

East Anglia, probably Suffolk; dated 1608; unidentified maker

Private Collection

With fig-shaped bowl and with slightly hexagonal stem and fluted baluster finial; engraved on top with initials TB below 1608; the back of the bowl engraved with simplified East Anglian decoration featuring fleurs-de-lis and a trapezoidal reservation enclosing the initials TN, with a zigzag border

The mark is identical to that struck on the spoon of St Peter Parmentergate Church, Norwich (no. 63)

L. 6⅝ in. (16.4 cm)

Mark: struck in bowl with a stylized fleur-de-lis or trefoil in beaded circular punch

1 This catalogue entry was prepared in collaboration with Timothy Kent.

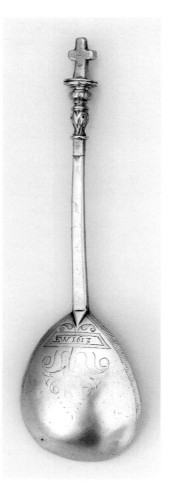

63

64

65

Seal-top spoon[1] *Silver, gilt*

East Anglia, probably Suffolk; dated 1600; unidentified maker

Private Collection

With fig-shaped bowl, tapering hexagonal stem and fluted baluster finial; the top engraved with initials IC *within simple scroll decoration and on back of stem* EA NATUS 1600

The engraving on the seal-disc is typically East Anglian. Similar marks appear on church plate in Suffolk, such as the paten of St Peter, Linstead Magna.[2]

L. 6⅞ in. (16.5 cm)

Mark: struck in bowl with probable maker's mark of a stylized fleur-de-lis or trefoil flanked by four pellets in beaded circular punch

Provenance: How of Edinburgh, from whom purchased by present owner, *c.*1990

1 This catalogue entry was prepared in collaboration with Timothy Kent.
2 SCP North Dunwich, *sub* Linstead Magna.

66

Seal-top spoon[1] *Silver, gilt*

East Anglia, probably Suffolk; dated 1609; unidentified maker

Private Collection

With fig-shaped bowl, tapering hexagonal stem and fluted baluster finial; the top engraved with initials IL *within simple scroll decoration and on back of stem* IH NATA MAY 5 ANO 1609

Undoubtedly by the same hand as the previous spoon and virtually identical in form and workmanship. The quality of both spoons is superior to most provincially made spoons. On both these spoons the initials engraved on the seal top are probably those of the godparent of the child whose initials and date of birth appear on the stem.

L. 6⅞ in. (16.5 cm)

Mark: struck in bowl with probable maker's mark of a stylized fleur-de-lis or trefoil flanked by four pellets in beaded circular punch

Provenance: Puchased in Grimsby from Leonard Hall and Son by a collector in 1940, from whose son acquired by the present owner in 1995

1 This catalogue entry was prepared in collaboration with Timothy Kent.

65

66

67

Seal-top spoon[1] *Silver, parcel-gilt*

Woodbridge; dated 1601; maker's mark probably that of
Robert Dale II (d. 1614)

Private Collection

*With fig-shaped bowl and with slightly tapering hexagonal stem,
with fluted baluster finial; the top engraved* WC *within simple
scrolls; the back of the bowl engraved with lozenges and
arabesques within a zigzag border and with initials* EG *and date
1601 within trapezoidal reservation*

Robert Dale II's will is dated January 29 1613/4. He describes
himself as "Robert Dale of Woodbridge in the County of
Suffolk, goldsmith". The will contains a reference to spoons
and he bequeaths to his sister's son, John Hunt, "a dossen of
silver spoones of the valew of tenne shillings a pece".[2] His
father, Robert Dale I, is recorded in Woodbridge in the 1568

search by the Wardens of the London Goldsmiths'
Company; in his will, dated September 10 1594, he bequeaths
his premises to his son Robert Dale II in remainder after
occupancy by his widow; his daughter Merable receives "one
feather bedde with the furniture thereunto belonging and
too paire of sheetes and also too silver spoones". Another
daughter Margaret, who had evidently been recently
married, also received two silver spoons together with six
pieces of pewter. His children Robert and Merable were
evidently under age at the time of his death as he instructs his
widow "to be careful for the bringing up of my said son and
daughter Robert and Merable in godly and good education
according to her ability and that my said son may be bound
within convenient time after my decease to some goode trade
with the good counsel and advice of my lovinge friend and
neighbour Nicholas Raby, gent."[3] We do not know where
Robert Dale II was apprenticed, but it may have been
Ipswich.

The engraving on the seal-disc is typically East Anglian.

L. 7 in. (17.8 cm)

Mark: Struck in bowl with maker's mark RD in circular
pelleted punch

1 This catalogue entry was prepared in collaboration with Timothy Kent.
2 Suffolk Record Office (Ipswich) 1C/AA1/50/13.
3 Suffolk Record Office (Ipswich) 1C/AA1/33/101.

68

Seal-top spoon[1] *Silver, traces of gilding on finial*

Waveney Valley, probably Beccles; *c*.1630; unidentified
maker

Private Collection

*With fig-shaped bowl, slightly hexagonal stem and fluted baluster
finial; the back of the stem with an incised trefoil (probably a
mark of ownership); the back of the bowl engraved with a lavish
panel of foliate scrolls, arabesques and freely-rendered fleurs-de-
lis, with vacant trapezoidal reservation and zigzag border*

The finial form is typically East Anglian. Similar marks
appear on church plate in the Waveney Valley such as on the
cup of St John the Baptist, Barnby,[3] and on a seal-top spoon

67   68

dated 1613 in the British Museum. A spoon with a similar mark and the same decorative features, dated 1606, was formerly in the Ellis Collection and sold at Sotheby's, London, November 13/14, 1935, lot 242.

L. 6¾ in. (17.2 cm)

Mark: struck in bowl with mark of nine pellets in circular beaded punch

Provenance: Anonymous sale, Christie's, New York, April 17, 1985, lot 419

1 This catalogue entry was prepared in collaboration with Timothy Kent.
2 SCP Lothingland, *sub* Barnby.

69

Seal-top spoon[1] *Silver, parcel-gilt*

Beccles; dated 1622; maker's mark probably that of Richard Chesten (fl. *c*.1615–1630)

Private Collection

With fig-shaped bowl and slightly tapering hexagonal stem with panels of engraved saltire decoration on both sides; the back and front of the bowl engraved with simple arabesques and lozenges; the centre of the back of the bowl engraved within a plain escutcheon a horse or donkey (probably an heraldic charge, a crest or possibly a badge); with very bold baluster seal the top pricked SF over 1622

The Chesten family were prominent goldsmiths in Beccles. In the London Company Search of 1593 Hamond Chesten[2] was found in possession of six spoons which were made of substandard silver. Another goldsmith member of this family was John Chesten who died in 1617,[3] with Richard Chesten, the maker of this spoon, as witness to his will.

This spoon, weighing some three ounces, is of exceptional size and weight and was obviously made to a special commission.

Another spoon with the same bowl mark RC and mullets is recorded in correspondence dating between 1915 and 1919 between members of the Fuller family of Kenninghall, Mrs Rachel H. Fuller of Tharston and a local auctioneer, Moore, Garrard & Son of Hoxne, in which it is described as "the old

69

family spoon". This spoon and the correspondence were in the possession of Mr P. Larner of St Albans in 1998.[3]

L. 7¾ (19.7 cm)

Marks: Struck once in bowl with maker's mark RC mullet above and below in circular punch and once on back of lower stem with further maker's mark RI.CH in serrated rectangular punch

Provenance: Gerald S. Sanders Collection (S71 in MS catalogue); How of Edinburgh, from whom purchased by the present owner *c*.1985

1 This catalogue entry was prepared in collaboration with Timothy Kent.
2 This name appears as "Harmon Ghosted" and in other incorrect forms in Jackson (p. 347) and elsewhere.
3 Beccles Parish Register (Suffolk Record Office, Ipswich).

The Waveney Valley

Goldsmiths are known to have been working in Beccles, Bungay, Diss and Harleston in the sixteenth and seventeenth centuries. The greatest concentration was in Beccles where some, such as the Chesten family, prospered from the demand for small silverwares from the area's yeomen farmers and merchants. More than thirty Suffolk churches have Elizabethan communion cups struck with variations of a quatrefoil, cinquefoil or sexfoil mark, the petals usually in the form of stylized radiating hearts.[1] This evidence has served to link similar marks found on spoons to the same area. Like the Bury St Edmunds fleur-de-lis, these marks do not appear to be the marks of individual makers but are perhaps best regarded as "symbols of quality", used by workshops in the Waveney Valley, and most probably in Beccles, between the 1560s and the middle of the seventeenth century.

In the 1690s Lionel Girling, originally from Yarmouth but who had trained in Norwich, set up shop in Beccles, where he was fined by the London goldsmiths' company for having substandard wares in 1703, 1705 and 1719.[2]

In Harleston, Henry Fen, perhaps related to the Fenn (or Fenne) family who made silver in Norwich in the previous century, is the only maker to whom a mark can be confidently attributed. Formed of a roman HF conjoined, it appears in conjunction with a variant of the four hearts mark and an unidentified mark which may be a death's head, on a paten at Pulham St Mary. The angular shield and pellets of Fen's maker's mark are similar to one of the marks used by Thomas Hutchinson of Great Yarmouth, suggesting they may have trained or worked together. Fen's mark also appears on a small two-handled saucer in the Ipswich Museum. Fen's death is recorded in 1688.

1 It should be borne in mind that similar marks are also recorded elsewhere, such as the mark of six radiating Vs found on the Elizabethan cup at Cheveley in Cambridgeshire.
2 Girling's mark, LG in a rectangle, occurs on its own on church plate in the area and is found in conjunction with Norwich hallmarks for 1691 on the cup and cover at Stockton, and overstriking Elizabeth Haslewood's mark on a beaker with Norwich hallmarks for 1697–8, sold Christie's, London, April 27, 1983, lot 187.

70

Communion cup *Silver*

Waveney Valley, probably Beccles; *c.*1570; unidentified maker

All Saints Church, Knettishall, Suffolk

On domed foot and waisted stem, the bell-shaped bowl with a horizontal band of engraved dashes

H. 4⅝ in. (11.7 cm); DIAM. 2¾ in. (7 cm); WEIGHT. 3 oz. 5 dwt (101 g)

Mark: Struck on rim with mark formed of six radiating hearts

Published: SCP *sub*, Blackburne, p. 284

Fig. 27 Mark from the seal-top spoon *c.*1580, no. 71

Fig. 28 Mark from the seal-top spoon *c.*1650, no. 74

Fig. 29 Marks attributed to Henry Fen of Harleston from a paten, Pulham St Mary, Norfolk

70

Spoons of the Waveney Valley

More spoons attributable to the Beccles area survive than from any other part of East Anglia with the exception of Norwich. The prosperity of the Waveney Valley, with its high proportion of merchants and independent yeomen, created great demand for the smaller wares of a silversmith's workshop. Elaborately decorated examples such as no. 69 are rare, but even this example shows the unmistakable characteristics of spoons from this area. They include a somewhat elongated terminal, usually with an extended cylinder between the baluster section and the distinctively dentilated cushion-shaped section under the seal top, and a comparatively slender stem. The discs at the end of the terminals on Beccles spoons are often of much smaller diameter than those found on Norwich spoons of the same period.

71

Seal-top spoon *Silver*

Waveney Valley, probably Beccles; *c*.1580; unidentified maker

Private Collection

With fig-shaped bowl, with tapering flat hexagonal stem and fluted baluster knop; the top engraved with the initials BT

L. 6¼ in. (15.8 cm)

The same mark is found on a seal-top spoon with a somewhat smaller terminal than the present example,[1] and on a maidenhead spoon.[2]

Marks: Struck on bowl with mark composed of four hearts set as a cross (Jackson, p. 347, line 1), see fig. 27, facing page

1 How, *Spoons*, vol. 1, p. 234.
2 Sold Christie's, South Kensington, April 20, 1999, lot 91.

72

Apostle spoon of St Peter *Silver*

Waveney Valley, probably Beccles; dated 1597; unidentified maker

The Ticktum Collection

With fig-shaped bowl and slightly tapering stem; the back of the bowl pricked with the initials IHCP *and date* 1597

L. 6⅞ in. (17.5 cm)

Marks: Struck in bowl with mark composed of four hearts set as a cross each containing three pellets (Jackson, p. 347, line 2)

73

Seal-top spoon *Silver, parcel-gilt*

Waveney Valley, probably Beccles; *c*.1630–50; unidentified maker

Private Collection

With fig-shaped bowl, with tapering flat hexagonal stem and fluted baluster hexagonal knop; the top pricked with the initials RP *over* TC

L. 6¼ in. (15.8 cm)

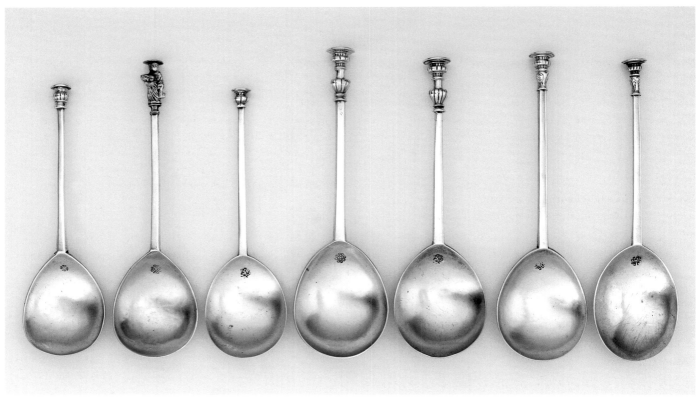

Left to right 71–77

Marks: Struck in bowl with mark composed of four hearts set as a cross each containing three pellets (Jackson, p. 347, line 2)

Provenance: Anonymous sale, Woolley & Wallis, Salisbury, July 25, 2003, lot 319

74
Seal-top spoon *Silver*

Waveney Valley, probably Beccles; dated 1650; unidentified maker

The Ticktum Collection

With fig-shaped bowl, with tapering flat hexagonal stem and fluted baluster knop; the top engraved with the initials MA over MP over 1650

L. 7 in. (17.8 cm)

Marks: Struck in bowl with mark composed of four hearts set as a cross each containing three pellets (Jackson, p. 347, line 2), see fig. 28, p. 92

75
Seal-top spoon *Silver*

Waveney Valley, probably Beccles; dated 1658; unidentified maker

Private Collection

With fig-shaped bowl, with tapering flat hexagonal stem and fluted baluster knop; the top engraved with the initials GS over RS over 1658

The terminal on this spoon and the previous one, no. 74, are clearly from the same mould.

L. 6⅞ in. (17.5 cm)

Marks: Struck in bowl with mark composed of four hearts set as a cross each containing three pellets (Jackson, p. 347, line 2)

76

Seal-top spoon *Silver*

Waveney Valley, probably Beccles; *c.*1650; unidentified maker

Private Collection

With fig-shaped bowl, with tapering flat hexagonal stem and fluted baluster knop; the top engraved with the initials WH *over* WS *over* 16?

L. 7 in. (17.8 cm)

Marks: Struck in bowl with mark composed of four hearts set as a cross each containing three pellets (Jackson, p. 347, line 2)

77

Seal-top spoon *Silver*

Waveney Valley, probably Beccles; first half of the seventeenth century; unidentified maker

Private Collection

*With fig-shaped bowl, with tapering flat hexagonal stem and fluted baluster knop; the top engraved c.*1800 *with the initials* IG

L. 6⅞ in. (17.5 cm)

Marks: Struck in bowl with mark composed of four hearts each containing three pellets (Jackson, p. 347, line 2)

Provenance: Anonymous sale, Christie's, South Kensington, November 10, 1998, lot 118, private collection

78

Baluster-knop spoon *Silver*

Probably Beccles; *c.*1620; maker's mark probably that of Richard Chesten (fl. *c.*1615–1630)

Private Collection

With egg-shaped bowl and slightly tapering stem, with fluted baluster and plain flange to the knop; the reverse of the bowl engraved with the initials WS *over* B *by the base of stem and below that with the initials* B.O; *the front engraved with the initials* SN *flanking the mark*

For remarks about the Chesten family, see no. 69.

L. 6⅝ in. (16.8 cm)

Marks: Struck in bowl with maker's mark RC mullet above and below in circular serrated punch

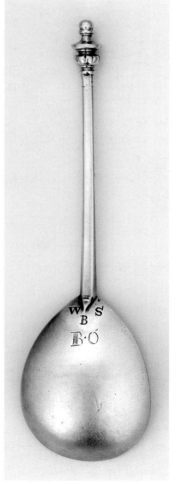

78

Great Yarmouth

79

Communion cup *Silver*

Great Yarmouth; *c.*1680; maker's mark of Thomas Hutchinson (fl. *c.*1675–1699)

St Mary's Church, Bungay, Suffolk

On domed spreading flat foot and spool-shaped stem with moulded band, the deep bowl with everted sides, engraved BUNGAY SAINT MARY'S

In 1568, the churchwardens of St Mary's church had purchased a new communion cup and cover "made of one paire of chalice", paying an additional 21s "for some sylv'". The cup was apparently stolen in 1682, for in that year the churchwardens' accounts list[1]:

> Pd. For a warrant & expenses in finding the old
> plate that Was stolen   00-02-06

The cup may have been recovered in a damaged state for the accounts also record:

> Pd. To Mr Hutchinson for a new communion cup
> the old One being discounted   02-11-04

The most likely Hutchinson is Thomas Hutchinson of Great Yarmouth. He had several apprentices and is last mentioned in 1699, when his son and apprentice, John Hutchinson, was admitted a freeman of Yarmouth.

Hutchinsons are recorded as goldsmiths in Norwich, Colchester and Chelmsford as well as Great Yarmouth during the second half of the seventeenth century and they were probably all related. A Thomas Hutchinson of Chelmsford was fined by the London company in 1622 for seven substandard spoons.[2] Another Thomas, presumably his son, was described as "the elder, of Chelmsford in the County of Essex, goldsmith" in his will dated 12 August 1651. In it he left legacies to his sons Thomas, William, Richard and Edward.[3] Daniel Hutchinson was admitted a freeman of Norwich by purchase in 1661,[4] and was fined for some small offence at the View of Frankpledge in the ward of St Peter Mancroft in 1675.[5] He died in 1685 and was

buried in St Andrew's Church, Norwich. A Richard Hutchinson was admitted a freeman of Norwich in 1736.

The same marks are found on the spoon, no. 80, and other versions appear on nos. 81 and 82.

H. 7¼ in. (18.3 cm); DIAM. 3½ in. (9 cm); WEIGHT 8 oz. 10 dwt. (264 g)

Marks: Struck on rim with a flowerhead, TH conjoined in roman letters within pellets, and twice with the gothic upper-case letter G (Jackson, p. 344, line 2)

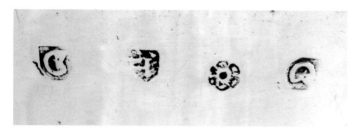

1 Mann, p. 73.
2 Goldsmiths' Company, Court Book P, part 2, p. 308.
3 PRO/PCC/PROB 11/218.
4 Freemen, Norwich, p. 70.
5 Barrett, *Norwich Silver*, p. 88.

80

Trefid spoon *Silver*

Great Yarmouth; dated 1676; maker's mark of Thomas Hutchinson (fl. *c*.1675–1699)

The Ticktum Collection

With egg-shaped bowl the back of which is die-struck with a pattern of stylized acanthus; with flat stem, the terminal pricked T over TM over 1676

These marks are recorded on several spoons[1] and on the communion cup of St Mary's, Bungay (no. 79) for which "Mr. Hutchinson" was paid £2 11s 4d in 1682.

L. 7¼ in (18.5 cm)

Marks: The stem struck with a flowerhead, TH conjoined in roman letters within pellets, and twice with the upper-case gothic letter G (Jackson, p. 334, line 2)

Provenance: H. D. Ellis Collection, Lieutenant-Colonel J. Benett-Stanford, Pythouse, Tisbury, Wiltshire, sale, Sotheby's, London, June 6, 1946, lot 107; The Paterson Collection, sale, Christie's, South Kensington, November 1998, lot 62, the Ticktum Collection

80   81

1 For example one from the H. D. Ellis Collection, sold, Sotheby's, London, November 13–14, 1935, lot 74. The preceding lot was another trefid with the same TH conjoined and flowerhead but with the gothic upper-case letter G reversed.

81

Spoon *Silver*

Great Yarmouth; *c*.1680; maker's mark of Thomas Hutchinson (fl. *c*.1675–1699)

The Ticktum Collection

With egg-shaped bowl; originally a trefid spoon (the terminal now removed)

Although only a fragment, this spoon is important because of the marks on the stem, which form one of several sets of similar marks known to have been used by Hutchinson. The same maker's mark appears on the porringer (no. 82) and should be compared with the similar marks of a flowerhead and G found in conjunction with another version of the maker's mark – TH conjoined in roman letters found on several spoons (see no. 80) and, most importantly, on the communion cup of St Mary's, Bungay ordered from "Mr. Hutchinson" in 1682 (no. 79). Most importantly, identical die-struck decoration is found on the back of the bowl of this spoon and one struck with the documented Hutchinson mark (no. 80) thus providing a link between the two very similar marks.

L. 6½ in. (16.4 cm)

Marks: The stem struck with a stylized flowerhead, TH conjoined in italic letters, and twice with upper-case gothic G

Provenance: Said to have been purchased in the mid-twentieth century by Mr Turner, auctioneer of Ipswich; anonymous sale, Phillips, St Ives, February, 1991, the Ticktum Collection

82

Two-handled cup *Silver*

Great Yarmouth; *c.*1680;
maker's mark of Thomas
Hutchinson (fl. *c.*1675–1699)
Private Collection

Of circular baluster form on flat base, with two scroll handles; pricked under the rim with the initials MP *within scrolls and below that, c.*1780, *with the initial* G

The same marks of TH in monogram and a flowerhead appear in conjunction with the letter G on a trefid spoon sold from the Ellis Collection, Sotheby's, London, November 13, 1935, lot 75, where it is noted that "these identical marks with a fleur-de-lis instead of the G occur on a porringer *c.*1670–80".

H. 3½ in. (9 cm); w. 5¾ (14.5 cm); D. 4 in. (10.1 cm);
WEIGHT 5 oz. 19 dwt. (186 g)

Marks: Struck under rim twice with fleur-de-lis in an octagonal punch and once with TH conjoined in italic letters and with stylized flowerhead in circular bordered punch

Provenance: Anonymous sale, Sotheby's, London, January 27, 1966, lot 138 (bt. Kaye); private collection

King's Lynn

The King's Lynn goldsmiths[1]

Brand Inglis

The town of Lynn was founded towards the end of the eleventh century by the bishop of Norwich, Herbert de Losinga. He founded the church of St Margaret and a priory, in fulfilment of a promise to Pope Pashal II, as penance for the various acts of simony that had marked his ascent of the ecclesiastical ladder. He also laid the foundations of an economic and commercial community by establishing a grant of a market and a fair.

The town was ideally sited to exploit trade both by road and sea. Until the Black Death the population grew steadily and by the early fourteenth century had probably reached some 5,700 inhabitants. Looking at the number of freemen who are listed as goldsmiths between 1300 and 1710 we see here a fairly typical pattern:

Time	Total freemen	Goldsmiths
1300–05	94	2
1342–70	266	10 [*sic*]
1371–1400	255	1
1401–30	206	3
1431–60	455	3
1461–90	274	2
1491–1520	388	0
1521–50	364	1
1551–80	504	6
1581–1610	438	6
1611–40	452	3
1641–70	605	1
1671–1710	635	4

At first there is a steady number of goldsmiths during the Middle Ages, falling around the late fourteenth and early fifteenth centuries owing to successive and economically disastrous outbreaks of plague; rising until the mid-sixteenth century, and then waning steadily throughout the seventeenth.

It is really impossible to know how much work the medieval goldsmiths did, as there is virtually nothing left now for us to estimate the quantity—or quality—of their output, but it seems reasonable to suppose that they fulfilled a need much as the goldsmiths of the latter half of the sixteenth century did, as suppliers of fair to middling plate for the churches and monasteries in their area and as repairers and small-workers.

In Norfolk particularly there are large numbers of pre-Reformation patens surviving, mostly unmarked, which seem almost certain to have been made in one of the towns within the county. Take for instance the list of the plate from St Nicholas in Lynn sold in 1543:

1 little Crosse of silver	xvi [ounces]
1 little Crosslet of silver	
1 little cruett of silver gilt	x
1 cruett of silver gilt	viii
1 Pair Censors Gilt	xxxvii
1 Crucifix of silver gilt	xv
1 Scrip of silver	x
1 Pyxe of silver gilt	xxx
1 Broken Cross of silver pt gilt	xxiii
1 picture of Christ crucified	iii
2 knoppes of silver gilt	xvi
1 pyxe gilt	xxi
4 pyxes gilt	xvi
1 Chalice cover gilt	x
4 pattens silver gilt }	Lxxviii
4 chalices of silver gilt }	
1 Scepter part plate	ii
1 Chalice silver Patten gilt	xiii
1 Holy water stoop with a sprinkler	Lxxxx
1 Chalice silver with Paten gilt	xLiii

It seems unlikely that this large amount of plate was all made in London. Assuming the plate was accumulated over many years, it is significant that between 1415 and when the plate was sold in 1543, no fewer than eight goldsmiths were working in Lynn. Surely there would not have been so many were it not for local church patronage.

The period of religious disruption in the 1540s and 1550s must have been very bad for the local goldsmith. At the time

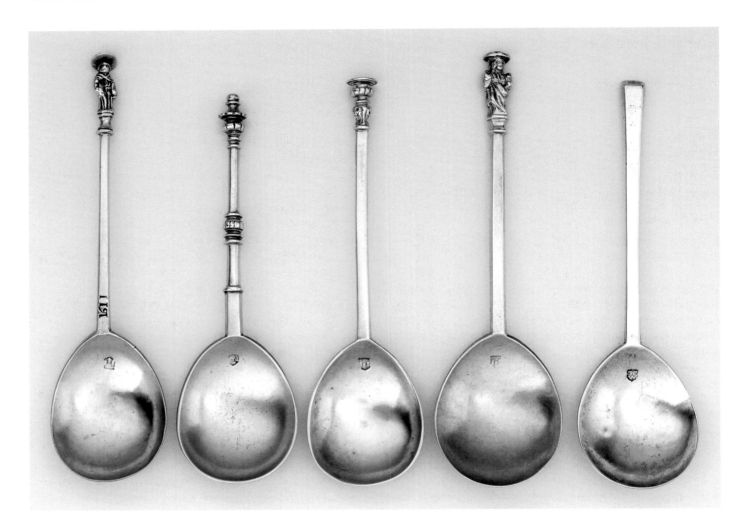

Fig. 30 King's Lynn spoons: left to right: St Matthew, c.1580, maker's mark probably that of Thomas Cooke (cat. no. 83); baluster-stem spoon c.1620, maker's mark of James Wilcocke (cat. no. 86); seal-top spoon dated 1611, possibly by James Wilcocke (cat. no. 85); St John, c.1620, maker's mark of James Wilcocke (cat. no. 87); slip-top spoon, c.1630, maker's mark possibly of William Howlett (cat. no. 89).

of the Dissolution of the Monasteries and later of the commissioners' reports on church goods, nervous churchmen would not have given large orders to the smiths. This is borne out by the list of Lynn freemen, which in the years from 1491 to 1550 contains only one goldsmith. King's Lynn's changing economic and ecclesiastical conditions clearly had an impact on the number of working goldsmiths.

The accession of Elizabeth I marked the beginning of a long period of full employment for the local goldsmiths, and the Lynn men were undoubtedly there in force to take what they could of the new orders forthcoming after the Queen's

proclamation of 22 March 1559 restoring the cup to the laity. The turn of the Norwich diocese seemingly came in 1566/7. In that year Lynn had four goldsmiths available to wrest as many orders as they could from their Norwich and London competitors. I have so far found seven cups by one Lynn maker, some of which bear engraved dates corresponding to that year, but I have been unable to trace which of the four goldsmiths it could have been.

The cups bearing this mark, which looks like a leaf over a circle enclosing the letter I (fig. 31), though neither beautiful nor well executed, are fairly representative of Elizabethan communion cups. A second group of slightly later Elizabethan pieces bears a single mark which could be TC conjoined and ascribable to Thomas Cooke (see fig. 32).

The communion cup at Fring, about twelve miles northeast of Lynn, is obviously Elizabethan though altered later. It has a rather strange mark, which I take to be a battle-axe

Fig. 31 Mark found on communion cups in the Lynn area, used by William Lonyson, Giles Walworth, Richard Waterman, or Lawrence de Wytte

Fig. 32 Mark possibly TC conjoined, possibly for a member of the Cooke family

Fig. 33 Mark of a battle axe, from the communion cup of Fring, Norfolk, here attributed to Thomas Bolden (fl. c.1556–after 1569)

(fig. 33). Since no other piece has come to my notice bearing this mark, the suggestion that it was made in Lynn can only be speculative, but there was a smith working in Lynn called Thomas Bolden and the mark might be a pun on his last name.

Another sixteenth-century goldsmith to whom I have ascribed a mark with more certainty is James Wilcocke (no. 84). He was made a freeman in 1593 and was still working in 1635. Wilcocke may have been prolific, but so far only two cups and one large gilt paten cover that were unquestionably made by him have come to light. He may have been the first to use the town mark of Lynn (three dragons' heads erect each pierced with a cross crosslet) along with his own maker's mark, IW, mullet above and below, but see Colin Ticktum's essay below. The communion cup and cover at Congham, although it does not bear Wilcocke's personal mark, is struck with the Lynn mark that he used and I believe is almost certainly made by him. There is also a small paten and three spoons that may be ascribed to him. His work displays sensitivity, sophistication and an awareness of contemporary London styles.

It must be assumed that some of the church wardens in the Lynn area had been rather dilatory in converting their old chalices into communion cups in 1567 because there are a fair number of cups by William Howlett dating from after Bishop White's visitation of 1629. Howlett was a competent craftsman, as the diversity of his work shows, but what is puzzling is the even greater diversity of quality and the way he appears to have cannibalized older pieces of silver in making some of his works. A few pieces made by Howlett have been recorded bearing the full London hallmarks of 1638 but what made him suddenly decide to take or send his silver to London to be marked remains a mystery. He was certainly

the most productive of all the Lynn makers judging by the amount of his work still extant. He used as a maker's mark H over W, and a Lynn mark similar to that used by James Wilcocke. On certain pieces he used a third mark formed of the letters ST in monogram, the S being reversed (no. 88). Almost certainly ST stands for sterling and affirms the standard of the silver. The fourth mark Howlett occasionally used is a unicorn's head incuse.

Robert Howlett, who was possibly the grandson of William Howlett, was made free as a goldsmith in 1661. The last mark for which I have a tentative identification appears on three silver alms dishes, all in churches within five miles of Lynn. They bear the mark RM and were probably made in the workshop of a goldsmith known simply as Mr Marsh, active in the late seventeenth and early eighteenth century. Crudely executed, they were surely not made in London. One other rather remote possibility is that they are by Richard Marsh, working in Ipswich in 1683.

Of the total output of the Lynn goldsmiths over a period of about 140 years fewer than fifty pieces are known to have survived.

1 This is a shortened version of a paper that first appeared in the *Proceedings of the Silver Society*, vol. 2, part 7, 1972, and is reprinted with kind permission of the editor. More information will be found in the catalogue *Lynn Silver*, King's Lynn.

The introduction of the King's Lynn town mark and the work of Thomas Cooke

Colin Ticktum

Seldom does a piece of silver come to light that forces us to review long established thinking. For many years it has been thought that the two distinct versions of the King's Lynn town mark found on silver of the first half of the seventeenth century were used either by the workshop of James Wilcocke or that of William Howlett. On some of the six recorded King's Lynn spoons and on various pieces of church plate, these two town marks appear either alone or in conjunction with Wilcocke's or Howlett's marks. When either of the town marks has appeared alone the object has been attributed to one or other workshop according to the version of the mark. The spoon, no. 83, requires us to revise our thinking about this.

This spoon is struck with the version of the town mark usually associated with James Wilcocke, but it is also struck with a hitherto unrecorded maker's mark that can be read as TC conjoined. The spoon has an incised date of 1611 on the

Fig. 34 Mark found in conjunction with the Lynn town mark on the spoon no. 83, here attributed to Thomas Cooke (fl. *c*.1578–?)

front of the stem but can probably be dated to the latter half of the sixteenth century. Our old assumption that James Wilcocke was responsible for the introduction of the King's Lynn town mark now needs to be revised. James Wilcocke was not free until 1593 and William Howlett not until 1629. Could the maker's mark on the spoon be that of Thomas Cooke?

Knowledge about the silversmith Thomas Cooke is scant. He was working before 1578 but we do not have his birth and apprenticeship dates. We do know that he was sworn into the trade by a visiting party of searchers of the London goldsmiths' company in 1578 and that he was fined. However, his freedom by purchase is not registered until 1579. He was therefore working some fourteen years before Wilcocke.

It could be that James Wilcocke was in fact Thomas Cooke's apprentice. With a gap of fourteen years between their freedom dates, this does not seem unreasonable. James Wilcocke may have taken over the workshop or in some way carried on Thomas Cooke's business. To do so was quite a common practice and is seen not only in London but also in the provinces up to the middle of the eighteenth century. However, what is crucial is that they both used the same version of the King's Lynn town mark.

Traditionally, a completely different mark has been given to Thomas Cooke, taken from church pieces dated around 1580 (see fig. 32).[1] This discovery calls into question that attribution. It is unlikely that Thomas Cooke would have had two marks, especially two that are of such a different form. Whether there are any other pieces with a possible TC conjoined mark which may come to light now that this information is published is something which might now be hoped for.

1 *Lynn Silver*, King's Lynn, p. 16 and Jackson, p. 346.

83

Apostle spoon of St Matthew *Silver, gilt*

King's Lynn; *c*.1580; maker's mark probably that of Thomas Cooke (fl. *c*.1578–?)

The Ticktum Collection

With fig-shaped bowl and tapering stem, the figure with rayed nimbus, the front stamped 1611

This hitherto unrecorded King's Lynn spoon is discussed in Colin Ticktum's essay, pp. 101–102.

L. 7¼ in. (18.2 cm)

Marks: Struck in bowl with town mark usually associated with James Wilcocke of three dragon's heads erect each pierced with a cross crosslet (*Lynn Silver*, King's Lynn, p. 16) and on back of stem with maker's mark ?TC conjoined in roman letters (fig. 34)

Provenance: Anonymous sale, Bonhams, London, April 15, 2003, lot 380; the Ticktum Collection

83

84

Mark: Struck on side of bowl with town mark of three dragon's heads erect each pierced with a cross crosslet and maker's mark IW mullet above and two below (*Lynn Silver*, King's Lynn, p. 16)

Published: NA, Norwich, pp. 107–8; *Lynn Silver*, King's Lynn, p. 22, no. 16

Exhibited: Lynn Silver, King's Lynn, 1972, no. 16, lent by St Peter Southgate Church, Norwich

1 Freemen, Lynn, p. 125.

85

Seal-top spoon *Silver*

King's Lynn; dated 1611; possibly by James Wilcocke (fl. 1593–after 1635)
The Ticktum Collection

With fig-shaped bowl, tapering hexagonal stem and fluted baluster finial; the top engraved 1611 *over* WR *over* LS

This spoon is struck with the version of the Lynn town mark usually found in conjunction with Wilcocke's maker's mark, suggesting an attribution to his workshop, but see pp. 101–102. The communion cup at Congham is similarly struck with the town mark but with no maker's mark.

L. 6¾ in. (7.1 cm)

Mark: Struck in bowl with the town mark of three dragon's heads erect each pierced with a cross crosslet (*Lynn Silver*, King's Lynn, p. 16)

Provenance: How of Edinburgh Ltd., London, anonymous sale, Woolley & Wallis, Salisbury, October 25, 2000, lot 10

Published: Lynn Silver, King's Lynn, p. 45, no. 61

Exhibited: Lynn Silver, King's Lynn, 1972, no. 61, lent anonymously

84

Cup *Silver*

King's Lynn; *c.*1620; maker's mark of James Wilcocke (fl. 1593–after 1635)
St Peter Southgate Church, Norwich

With flaring plain bowl on cast baluster stem and spreading foot

This is a typical secular goblet that perhaps at a later date was presented to the church for use as a communion cup. This would probably explain the presence of a King's Lynn piece in a Norwich church. James Wilcocke was free by purchase in 1593[1] and appears to have been working up to 1635.

H. 5¼ in. (13 cm); DIAM. 3⅜ in. (8.6 cm); WEIGHT 5 OZ. (156 g)

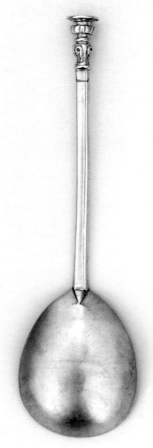

85

86

86

Spoon[1] *Silver, gilt*

King's Lynn; *c.*1620; maker's mark of James Wilcocke
(fl. 1593–after 1635)
Private Collection

With original gilding, the fig-shaped bowl and slightly tapering stem cast in sections, with central fluted knop and fluted baluster finial; engraved on reverse of bowl with initials AG

Similar stems, with balusters and knops separated by longer plain sections, are found on Dutch spoons of the period.[2] An early sixteenth-century Flemish painting of the Magi in the church of São Roque, Lisbon includes a spoon with almost identical decoration. While this spoon appears to be unique among English examples, it has features which identify it as English – and specifically East Anglian – apart

from its mark. Engraved initials on spoons were somewhat more common on spoons from this region than in the West Country,[3] the other main producer of spoons in Britain. Moreover this spoon has a typically English bowl and, unlike a Dutch spoon of the period, this bowl and stem are made in the English method of hammering out as one piece.

L. 6½ in. (16.5 cm)

Mark: struck in bowl with maker's mark IW mullet above and two below (*Lynn Silver*, King's Lynn, p. 16)

1 This catalogue entry was prepared in collaboration with Timothy Kent.
2 For example, one made in Zierkzee in 1616 illustrated in Frederiks, p. 14, no. 40, plate 27 and another Rotterdam, 1621, in the Museum Boymans-van Beuningen, illustrated in ter Molen, p. 508, no. 253.
3 See pp. 85–6.

87

Apostle spoon of St John *Silver*

King's Lynn; *c.*1620; maker's mark of James Wilcocke
(fl. 1593–after 1635)
Private Collection

*With fig-shaped bowl and slightly tapering stem; the back of the
bowl pricked FP*

L. 7⅜ in. (18.6 cm)

Marks: Struck in bowl with town mark of three dragon's
heads erect each pierced with a cross crosslet and on the back
of the stem with maker's mark IW mullet above and two
below (*Lynn Silver*, King's Lynn, p. 16)

Provenance: Gerald S.
Sanders Collection, How of
Edinburgh, from whom
purchased by Christine
Winfield in 1975,
The Winfield Collection,
Bonhams & Brooks, London,
March 6, 2001, lot 99, private
collection

Published: Lynn Silver, King's
Lynn, p. 45

Exhibited: Lynn Silver, King's
Lynn, 1972, no. 59 (lent by
G. S. Sanders)

87

88

88

Communion cup and paten-cover *Silver*

King's Lynn; dated 1633; maker's mark of William Howlett
(fl. *c.*1629–after 1653)
All Saints Church, Weasenham, Norfolk

*The cup on spreading reeded foot rising to a waisted stem with a
central small reeded knop, the flaring bowl engraved with two
horizontal bands of overlapping leaves enclosing:* FOR THE
PARRISH CHVRCH OF WESAM ALL SAINTS, ANNO DOM.
1633; *the cover plain with spool-form foot*

Cup: H. 6¾ in. (7.2 cm); DIAM. 3¼ in. (8.2 cm);
WEIGHT 6 oz. (187 g)
Paten-cover: H. 1¼ in. (3.1 cm); DIAM. 4¼ in. (10.7 cm);
WEIGHT 2 oz. 6 dwt. (72 g)

Marks: Struck on rim of cup and border of cover with town mark of three dragon's heads erect each pierced with a cross crosslet, ?standard mark ST (reversed) conjoined and with maker's mark (*Lynn Silver*, King's Lynn, p. 17, line 1)

Published: Lynn Silver, King's Lynn; NA Fincham, XXIII, p. 28

Exhibited: Lynn Silver, King's Lynn, 1972, no. 20

89

Slip-top spoon *Silver*

King's Lynn; *c.*1630; maker's mark possibly that of William Howlett (fl. 1629–*c.*1650)
Private Collection

With fig-shaped bowl and with hexagonal stem slightly tapering towards the bowl

The mark struck on this spoon appears to be a variation of the H over W mark found on church plate in the King's Lynn area which has been convincingly attributed to William Howlett by Gilchrist and Inglis.[1]

L. 7 in. (17.7 cm)

Mark: Struck in bowl with maker's mark H flanked by two pellets over W in shaped punch (cf. *Lynn Silver*, King's Lynn, p. 17)

1 *Lynn Silver*, King's Lynn, p. 17.

89

Bury St Edmunds

Notes on the silversmiths of Bury St Edmunds, 1550–1665

Wynyard Wilkinson

That silver is produced wherever there is wealth is one of the basic tenets of any examination of the history of the craft. It would therefore appear unlikely that the early economy of Bury St Edmunds could have sustained any significant silver trade. Indeed, even today's visitor to Bury encounters a prosperous yet modest market town easily eclipsed by nearby Cambridge or Newmarket. But it was not always thus. In the medieval world, the status of St Edmund, a king of the East Angles who had been killed whilst defending his realm against the invading Danes in 869, was such that pilgrims from all corners of Britain, as well as many from Europe, flocked to his shrine to pray and make offerings to the Abbey as keeper of the shrine.

The Abbey at Bury St Edmunds became as indispensable a destination to the medieval pilgrim as any of the great pilgrimage churches of the Continent. Consequently, the town enjoyed riches at a very early date. Along with access to this great wealth, the abbot of St Edmunds was granted almost absolute power over the Abbey and its environs, and the precinct was given unique and unprecedented exemption from secular rule.[1] It is for this reason that Bury St Edmunds does not appear in the Doomsday Book.

The civic growth and development which normally follow prosperity were largely denied Bury St Edmunds by its succession of all-powerful abbots, who were intent on maintaining an increasingly reactionary stranglehold on the town. Naturally, an abbot with absolute control over a burgeoning population was a recipe for conflict. It was not until 1606, when Letters Patent were granted establishing a secular government for the town, that normal civic government was installed in the town.

There is evidence of a small group of goldsmiths working at Bury St Edmunds at least as early as the tenth century.[2] The rise of the Abbey and its immense wealth ensured that there was sufficient work to sustain the trade throughout the medieval period. But it was after the suppression of the Abbey and all other monasteries in England that a period of unprecedented productivity for the silversmiths of Bury St Edmunds, and elsewhere, began.

The massing chalices of the old service were not suitable for the "group" Holy Communion of the new and in 1567 it was decreed by the Archbishop of York that all massing chalices in Bury St Edmunds and the rest of Suffolk were to be converted into communion cups. It was this decree that ensured that the work produced by the silversmiths of Bury St Edmunds would not fade into obscurity. Unlike the quotidian secular work of the early provincial silversmith that is lost, altered, or destroyed over time, post-Reformation communion cups in particular are important to scholarship because they *survive*.

By then, Bury St Edmunds' once thriving cloth-making industry had begun to decline, so the early merchant class to whom the local silversmiths would have catered was on the wane. Transforming church plate filled the void.

Bury's silversmiths seem to have remained a small close-knit group of artisans bound together by either familial or professional ties, or both. Thus, John Wether (d. 1568)[3] was apprenticed to Michael Hawkyn (d. 1559),[4] his uncle. John Wether's will was witnessed by his former apprentice and apparent successor, Erasmus Cooke (d. 1590).[5] Erasmus Cooke's daughter married Robert Ignes (d. 1631),[6] who seems to have succeeded his father-in-law upon the latter's death in 1690. Robert Ignes's nephew, Henry Tiler (d. 1664),[7] succeeded him. This one example represents a continuum of over a hundred years.

There is no evidence of more than two workshops ever operating simultaneously in Bury St Edmunds. Whereas from c.1200 to 1540 there appears to have been one workshop in continuous operation under a succession of masters, by 1560, there were at least two masters at work in Bury, together with their journeymen and apprentices. The two workshops seem to have expanded to absorb additional workers in good times, taking advantage of the Europe-wide journeyman system of casual labour by skilled artisans, and

Fig. 35 Jug with bridge spout, Raeren salt-glazed stoneware, silver mounts, probably Bury St Edmunds, *c*.1580. *Museum of Fine Arts, Boston, Theodora Wilbour Fund in Memory of Charlotte Beebe Wilbour (62.1166).*

"downsized" during leaner periods. Until the Letters Patent of 1606, workers from abroad were freely employed in Bury St Edmunds. Indeed, the tradition of encouraging the employment of foreign craftsmen was longstanding in the town, originating with the Abbot Baldwin, himself a Frenchman, physician to both Edward the Confessor and William the Conqueror, who took control of the Abbey in 1065, after leaving the Monastery of St Denis near Paris.[8] Therefore, it comes as no surprise that in the late 1560s, we find one James Stalker, an Edinburgh-trained goldsmith, working as a journeyman for Erasmus Cooke,[9] a local

goldsmith, probably because of the sudden increase in demand for communion cups. Indeed, in 1568 there were at least seven trained goldsmiths, many probably working as journeymen, recorded in Bury.

From surviving wills of various Bury St Edmunds goldsmiths, it is apparent that those of the 16th and early 17th centuries were flourishing tradesmen who owned much property and died possessed of impressive cash wealth. Men such as Robert Oliver (d. 1571 – his workshop continuing under his widow),[10] Erasmus Cooke, and Robert Ignes,[11] were successful retailers, who ran highly flexible and profitable businesses and were typical representatives of the new wealthy Tudor and Stuart merchant class. They were manufacturers in their own right, not simply retailers who purchased stock in London. However, London did hold a clear stylistic influence over these goldsmiths, and a fair amount of "wholesale" merchandise was bought there. London was also clearly considered the arbiter of matters professional even for the provincial goldsmiths. Records show that provincial goldsmiths swore allegiance as soon as they were able to the London goldsmiths' company, submitting to its rules and regulations, and many apprenticed their children to members of the London trade. For example, Simon Cooke, son of Erasmus, and inheritor of his father's tools, was apprenticed to the London goldsmith Rafe Bal in 1592.[12]

Whether they liked it or not, provincial goldsmiths were bound by certain rules set by the London company, who were charged by Parliament to implement the various acts and statutes relating to goldsmithing throughout the land. The archives of the Worshipful Company of Goldsmiths in London are indispensable when studying even the most obscure provincial makers, for they contain reports of the frequent spot checks conducted by the London wardens on provincial workers.

There are two occasions of particular interest wherein such unannounced "searches" were conducted in Bury St Edmunds. In 1568, a search revealed that Robert Oliver and Erasmus Cooke[13] were both found with substandard goods in their stock. Interestingly, one of the substandard pieces in Oliver's possession was a communion cup (not

Fig. 36 Incuse fleur-de-lis mark, probably of Bury St Edmunds on silver mounts of jug in fig. 35.

surprising, given the date). Given the significance of communion cups to Bury goldsmiths, one might assume that perhaps the original Catholic massing chalice from which Oliver's (only substandard) cup was re-fashioned was itself substandard, or much repaired, in which case the high solder content would have rendered the alloy below the required 92 per cent purity. Alternatively, this was a cup newly made from raw material that was below sterling standard. In any case, the London wardens took a lenient view, describing Robert Oliver as "seeming a man ancient in gravity and honesty."[14] That Robert Oliver's business survived this brief embarrassment is borne out in records showing his son inheriting the business at the age of twenty-four upon his mother's death.[15] In another instance, a list of the substandard merchandise held by the working goldsmiths Robert Ignes and Nicholas Ward during the 1629 great annual Bury fair at St Matthew's tide included all manner of small articles. The most interesting and unusual of these was the silver spectacle wire found in Ignes's shop.[16]

It is also from the London goldsmiths' company records taken during their "searches" that we learn many crucial details of the provincial silver trade which serve in the eventual work of attribution. In one entry, we discover the identity and nationality of temporary workers like James Stalker, the Scot who was working as a journeyman for Erasmus Cooke. In those searches revealing substandard goods we learn the precise nature of the provincial silversmith's wares. In the case of Nicholas Ward, the "heads" of his spoons were found to be "worse than the bodies".[17] Robert Ignes's spectacle wire tells us that silver-framed eyeglasses were being made in the English countryside as early as the 1620s.

By the mid seventeenth century, however, the fortunes of Bury's goldsmiths had changed. The untimely death of Henry Tiler, "in harness" in 1664 necessitated that an accurate inventory of his possessions be taken for tax and inheritance purposes. This meticulous document provides us with a precise inventory of the holdings typical of the provincial silversmith of the 1660s. As the last link in our continuum of Bury goldsmiths, he was the least wealthy, being farthest removed in time from the peak of Bury's silver production. In his shop at the time of his death were:

> *1 silver tankard*
> *2 footed beer bowls*
> *1 footed wine bowl*
> *1 tumbler*
> *2 sugar dishes*
> The total weight of the above items was fifty-four ounces.

The inventory continues:

> *3 plain tumblers*
> *1 salt*
> These weighed sixty ounces.

Also included in the inventory are:

> *5 spoons*
> *3 gilt bowls*
> *1 casting bottle*
> *A quantity of thimbles*
> " " " *bodkins*
> " " " *corals (rattles)*
> " " " *small boxes*
> " " " *buttons*
> " " " *tobacco stoppers*
> " " " *seals*
> *1 silver hourglass case*

A notation indicates the modest nature of Henry Tiler's business in that the sum of just £2 is due to his estate for unpaid goods. Therefore, Tiler's trade was apparently not robust enough to allow him to extend credit to his customers.[18]

There is much compelling evidence to ascribe a mark that appears to be a fleur-de-lis to Bury St Edmunds. This mark, an incuse one, survives mainly on spoons and communion cups, and very rarely on other pieces of domestic silver. There are over forty communion cups bearing fleur-de-lis marks, thirty-seven of which remain within a twenty-mile radius of Bury.

Why a fleur-de-lis would have become a mark associated with Bury St Edmunds is most likely explained in this way. Most silver objects were customarily made from melted coinage during the period in question. Because English coinage had been debased by order of Henry VIII in 1544 (the same year the sterling lion was introduced for English plate) and no longer contained the coin's value in silver, English goldsmiths began using French coinage to produce their wares. French coinage of the period was emblazoned with the fleur-de-lis and it is probable that it was used as the sign over the shop and workshop of the principal goldsmith in Bury St Edmunds over a period of at least 100 years.

This is but a brief survey of the early goldsmiths of Bury St Edmunds and the economic conditions under which they worked. The challenge of further discovery among the surviving records of the period remains.

1 Statham, p. 11.
2 Seaby, 1970, p. 63.
3 Bury St Edmunds Wills (W1/10/208).
4 London Goldsmiths' Minute Book.
5 P.C.C. Wills PROB 11/77.

90

6 Bury St Edmunds Wills.
7 Bury St Edmunds Inventories.
8 Statham, p. 26.
9 London Goldsmiths' Minute Book, 1569.
10 Bury St Edmunds Wills (WI/36/105).
11 The phonetic interpretations given to the goldsmith's names when they are being transcribed can be quite challenging to the researcher. Thus, Robert Ignes, for this is how he signed his own name, can be found mentioned in various records as "Hynes", "Hynds", "Hanes", "Innes", etc. One way to attempt to cope with these discrepancies is to try pronouncing the name in question whilst mimicking the local accent. Suddenly mistranscriptions make sense, and what were thought to be several people with similar names are in fact one and the same.
12 Provincial Apprentices Register.
13 London Goldsmiths' Minute Books.
14 Ibid.
15 Bury St Edmunds Wills (WI/36/105).
16 London Goldsmiths' Minute Books 1629.
17 Ibid.
18 Bury St Edmunds Inventories, 1664.

90

Communion cup and paten *Silver*

Bury St Edmunds; *c.*1570; unidentified maker
Private Collection

The cup with deep tapering bowl engraved with a horizontal band of four rows of dashes between double-ruled borders; on spool form stem with dentilation at top and bottom and domed circular foot; the paten circular with flat rim with ruled border and with dished centre

For a discussion of the significance of the fleur-de-lis see p. 109 of Wynyard Wilkinson's essay. While the fleur-de-lis appears on a broad range of silver of the sixteenth and seventeenth centuries found throughout Britain, the largest concentration is on church plate within a twenty-mile radius of Bury St Edmunds. The Bury variant is an incuse stamp and it has been recorded also on a handful of secular pieces (see fig. 35). The communion cups date from the period of the great chalice conversion programme of the 1560s and 1570s. Whether this fleur-de-lis mark was a form of standard or location mark used by more than one workshop, or an identifying mark of a particular maker, is uncertain.

Cup: H. 5 in. (12.6 cm); DIAM. 2¾ in. (7 cm)
Paten: DIAM. 3⅝ in. (8.4 cm)

Marks: Struck under lip of cup and on rim of paten with fleur-de-lis incuse

91

Communion cup *Silver*

Bury St Edmunds; *c.*1570; unidentified maker
Private Collection

The cup with deep tapering bowl engraved with a horizontal band of arabesques between double-ruled borders; on spool form stem with dentilation at top and bottom and domed circular foot attached to the stem by a flange without solder; the paten circular with flat rim with ruled border and with dished centre

H. 6¼ in. (16 cm); DIAM. 3½ in. (8.8 cm); WEIGHT 9 OZ. 13 dwt. (303 g)

Marks: Struck under lip with fleur-de-lis incuse

Provenance: Anonymous sale, Sotheby's, London, April 23, 1970, lot 148 (bt. Dodson); private collection

91

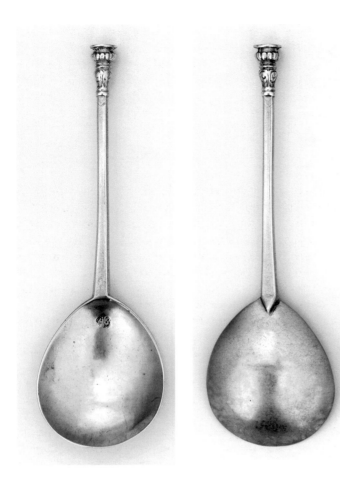

92

92

Seal-top spoon *Silver-gilt*

Possibly Bury St Edmunds; early seventeenth century;
unknown maker

The Ticktum Collection

*With fig-shaped bowl, tapering hexagonal stem and fluted
baluster finial*

L. 6¼ in. (16 cm)

Mark: struck in bowl with fleur-de-lis within a beaded
circular punch

Provenance: Christie's, South Kensington, May 1998

Ipswich and Colchester

Over forty communion cups exist in churches within a twenty-five mile radius of Ipswich struck with a single mark of a G in a shaped punch. This mark has prompted a considerable amount of debate over the years, and speculation whether it was a town or a maker's mark. Henry C. Casley, writing in 1904,[1] rejected Cripps' suggestion that it stood for "Gippeswic", the old name for Ipswich, as the goldsmiths of Ipswich do not appear to have been organized into any sort of guild or corporate body. Casley suggested another explanation, later supported by Brand Inglis, that the G was used by one or more members of the Gilbert family, who seem to have been the predominant family of goldsmiths in Ipswich in the sixteenth century. In 1544 the churchwardens of Mendlesham in Suffolk sold to "Gylbart ye gouldsmyth of Ipswch" most of their church plate.[2]

There were two Gilbert brothers: Richard, whose two sons became goldsmiths in Cheapside, London, and Jefferye. Richard appears to have died in 1543 and it is Jefferye who can be credited with producing many of the communion cups that replaced the old massing chalices in Ipswich area churches in the 1560s and 70s. His mark also appears on the magnificent tazza belonging to St Peter, Charsfield. This secular piece is similar to the Peterson cup (fig. 11) in Norwich.

In addition to the mark of a G, Gilbert appears to have used two others: JG in monogram, which appears on three cups, and a G in a heraldic shield, which appears once, on the cup belonging to St Mary Quay, Ipswich.[3]

Jefferye Gilbert married four times, first to Katherine, who was already the widow of two Ipswich goldsmiths, John Shoytt and Matthew Garrarde. By all four wives he had children; by his fourth wife, Katherine Symonds, whom he married in 1545, he had a son Lawrence who became a goldsmith. Jefferye Gilbert held a number of civic posts in Ipswich, including that of Chamberlain, as Peter Peterson did in Norwich. This position would effectively have enabled Gilbert to use civic funds as capital for his own business. In 1560 he served as Bailiff and, with a visit from Queen Elizabeth pending, when it was found that no coat of arms had ever been officially confirmed to the town, "John Gardyner and Jeffry Gilbert, bailiffs of the said Town of Ypswiche being uncerteyne of the aunciente armes belongine to theyre saide towne and corpora'con, and not willinge to do anything preiudiciall to any manner of person or persons hath instantly required Clarencieulx Kinge of Armes to make search in the registers and records of [his] office and to assigne unto them theyr right and aunciente arms".[4] Gilbert, a man of some considerable property, was buried on January 21, 1579 in St Lawrence's Church, Ipswich, under a stone slab that recorded "that he did beare the Mace before Queen Elizabeth of famous memory".[5]

Jefferye's son Lawrence, who would have been finishing his apprenticeship about the time that the chalice conversion programme began, appears to have been sent to open a shop in Colchester to fill orders for new communion cups in that area sometime in the mid 1560s. In 1567 he was visited there by the searchers of the London goldsmiths' company. The communion cup at Mark's Tey, dated 1567, is struck with a mark of a G pierced by an L in a shaped punch. The same mark appears on several cups in the Colchester area; it is also recorded on spoons and on the rare wine taster, no. 95, which was dredged out of the Thames. Lawrence also used another mark, a similar LG conjoined in an incuse die, which appears on the ostrich egg cup, no. 93. This highly decorated "cabinet" object, together with the severely plain wine taster, give an indication of the range and quality of Gilbert's output. By 1573 Lawrence seems to have returned to Ipswich and carried on working there.

The Gilberts were by no means the only plateworkers in Ipswich. Jackson lists a steady stream of names, including, in 1557, William Myles who married one of Jefferye Gilbert's daughters. He was born in Berghen op den Zoom in 1515[6] and is recorded in 1575 as having a journeyman named Christopher Buttell who was doubtless related to Thomas Buttell of Norwich and Cambridge.[7] Martyn Denys, also mentioned in 1575, was also an immigrant worker, having been born in "Duysburghe, Duke of Cleves country", in 1494.[8] William Whitinge, first mentioned in 1609, may have used a mark of a W with a crown which appears on eight communion cups within a radius of ten miles of Ipswich, but the identity of the maker who used a wavy cross, or the mark BT, remains a mystery.

In Woodbridge, the workshop of the Dales, father and son, appears to have been prosperous in the reigns of Elizabeth and James I (see no. 67). In Sudbury John Goodwyn, goldsmith, is recorded in 1673,[9] but no mark has been attributed to him. The mark CM appears on several pieces of church plate in the deanery of Hoxne and may have been used by a Bury St Edmunds workshop.

The Hutchinson family appear as goldsmiths in Colchester and Chelmsford in the seventeenth century; the Colchester family went on to register marks in London well into the eighteenth century (see no. 96), and it is likely that they were related to the Hutchinsons who worked in Norwich and Great Yarmouth.

1 Casley, pp. 164–5.
2 Cox, p. 140.
3 SCP, *sub* Ipswich, p. 178.
4 Casley, p. 168.
5 Inglis, "Gilbert", p. 572.
6 Casley, p. 183.
7 Oman, *Church Plate*, p. 138.
8 Casley, p. 183.
9 Will proved at Bury, April 18, 1678.

93

Ostrich-egg cup[1] *Silver, gilt, ostrich egg*

Colchester; *c*.1570; maker's mark of Lawrence Gilbert (*c*.1546–after 1573)
Private Collection, United States

On domed circular base with ovolo border enclosing a band chased with alternate lion and demonic masks between clusters of exotic fruit; rising to a baluster stem applied with masks and a calyx of stylized acanthus leaves; the egg enclosed by four reeded vertical straps; the flaring rim decorated with a band of arabesque work within hatched interlacing strapwork above a band of styled acanthus

This is the only surviving provincial English ostrich-egg cup; it is evident, from a close comparison of some of the decorative motifs used on the mounts and with communion cups bearing Lawrence Gilbert's marks in churches within a twenty-mile radius of Colchester, that the cup was made in his workshop and is not a London-made cup retailed by him. Judging by the quality of most of the communion cups in the

Colchester area either bearing Gilbert's mark, or from shape and form obviously made by him, it is clear that the making of this ostrich egg cup would have been well within Lawrence Gilbert's capabilities. It is arguably one of the half-dozen most important pieces of English sixteenth-century silver made outside London still extant.

Ostrich eggs were believed to be the egg of the gripe, or griffin, and were highly prized and very expensive; indeed, in most cases, it is probable that the egg cost more than the mounts. In the collection of Elizabeth I there were, in 1574, at least three mounted ostrich eggs. This cup is a rare survival of one of the natural curiosities so beloved in sixteenth-century England. It is a non-functional object: it is doubtful if it was ever drunk from, not least because of the practical difficulty of making the rim-mount absolutely watertight.

H. 9½ in. (24 cm); GROSS WEIGHT 18 OZ. (559 g)

Marks: Struck on plate underneath base twice with maker's mark LG conjoined incuse

Provenance: John and Helena Hayward, Brand Inglis Ltd., private collection

Published: Inglis (1997), pp. 570–72

1 This catalogue entry is based on Brand Inglis' essay "An ostrich-egg cup by Lawrence Gilbert of Colchester" in *Silver Society Journal*, autumn 1997, pp. 570–72.

93

94

94

Communion cup *Silver*

Ipswich; *c.*1570; maker's mark of Jefferye Gilbert
(fl. *c.*1528–1579)
Private Collection

*The cup with deep tapering bowl with everted rim, engraved
with a horizontal band of arabesques between double-ruled
borders; on spool form stem headed by a band of dentilation with
domed circular foot*

H. 5⅛ in. (13 cm); DIAM. 3⅛ in. (7.9 cm)

Marks: Struck on lip with G in a shaped punch

Provenance: Spink and Son Ltd.;
private collection

95

Wine Taster[1] *Silver*

Colchester or Ipswich; *c.*1570–5; maker's mark of Lawrence
Gilbert (*c.*1546–after 1573)
The Albert Collection

*The taster is shaped similarly to the Bordeaux models – with
raked sides and a high domed base, resting on a cyma reversa and
concave moulded wire foot. It is devoid of a handle. It is deeply
engraved with the conjoined initials* TW *immediately adjacent
to the maker's mark*

The surface is degraded in a manner consistent with its
having been in the River Thames for a considerable period.
The taster was dredged from the Thames by a wharf known
as "Vintry" or "Three Cranes' close to Vintners" Hall –
where wine was unloaded coming into the Port of London.
In the sixteenth century a famous tavern there was called the
"Three Cranes in the Vintry". A century later this was a
favourite haunt of Ben Jonson. However, Samuel Pepys
visited it on January 23, 1661, and wrote of it: "We all went
over the Three Cranes Tavern and, though the best room in
the house, in such narrow dog-hole we were crammed and
I believe there were nearly forty, that it made me loathe my
company and victuals, and a very sorry poor dinner it was
too."

For many decades the earliest known English wine
taster was one of 1631.[3] The present taster now holds that
distinction.

DIAM. 3 in. (9.2 cm);
WEIGHT 2 oz 10 dwt. (78 g)

Mark: Double struck on side with
maker's mark LG conjoined

95

1 This catalogue entry, by Robin Butler, is reproduced from the recently published catalogue *The Albert Collection* (London, 2004), p. 268, by kind permission.

2 Jackson, p. 343.

3 However, about 1990 an example, then on loan to Bristol City Museum and Art Gallery from Lacock Parish Church, was found to date from 1603. It is now in a private collection.

96

Trefid spoon[1] *Silver*

Probably Colchester; *c.*1675; maker's mark probably that of Richard Hutchinson II (died 1680)

Private Collection

With heart-shaped bowl and wide flat stem showing original guidelines, engraved on front of terminal A *over* CK

This is an early type of trefid spoon. The attribution of this maker's mark to Hutchinson is based on the similarity between it and the mark entered at Goldsmiths' Hall by Richard Hutchinson of Colchester in 1727.[2] Grimwade's "Richard Hutchinson II" is probably in fact IV or V. A Richard Hutchinson, born in 1676 and evidently the son of Richard II, described as "late of Colchester in the County of Essex, was apprenticed to John Sutton, a prominent London goldsmith, on 17 December 1690.[3] He entered a mark as a largeworker at Goldsmiths' Hall in 1699, where he was described as "in Colchester". He was admitted a Free Burgess of Colchester in 1700 and appears to have been dead by 1701. The business appears to have been carried on by his son Richard who entered the new mark in 1727.[4] A Richard Hutchinson, goldsmith, was admitted a freeman of Norwich in 1736.[5] The Hutchinson family of silversmiths was widespread in East Anglia (cats. nos. 79–82).

The engraved (not pricked) initials on this spoon are typically East Anglian. Fleur-de-lis marks, although encountered elsewhere (e.g. the Peard family of Barnstaple and the Dodsons of Lewes) are found widely in East Anglia (see p. 72).

L. 8⅜ in. (21.5 cm)

Mark: struck on back of stem twice with fleur-de-lis in shaped square punch and once with maker's mark RH within quatrefoil punch

1 This catalogue entry was prepared in collaboration with Timothy Kent.

2 Grimwade, no. 3433.

3 Grimwade, p. 719.

4 *Essex Review*, vol. 60, no. 239, July 1951, pp. 162–3.

5 Freemen, Norwich, p. 71.

96

Cambridge silversmiths

A Goldsmiths' Row is mentioned as early as 1285 in Cambridge, close to the market-place in St Mary's parish, and ten years later, on May 6, 1285, a deed for property in the same parish mentions Mathew Goldsmith and Henry of Barton, goldsmith.[1] By the sixteenth century it appears that Goldsmiths' Row was located in St Benet's parish;[2] goldsmiths described as of that parish are mentioned in the churchwardens' accounts of Great St Mary's as early as 1540, when "a payar of silver bedes and 2 other payer of Corall gardyd with silver ware solde by ye churchwardens to James goldsmith of Seynct benett parish in presence of Mr. Robert Smythe by ye consent of most parte of ye parochioners" and "Item the colar or bandryk of gold havynge ix lynks enameled of gold with ye vch for Seynct Nicolas & lityll Monstre or Relock of Seynct Nicolas oyll ys taken fro ye custody of ye churchwardens to be sold at Sterbrige feyar be agreement & consent also of ye parochionors".[3]

The mention of Stourbridge Fair, the great fair held each Michaelmas on the outskirts of Cambridge, is significant, for it attracted goldsmiths from as far away as Norwich, offering not only "fairings" (i.e. small silver tokens, snuff- or comfit-boxes or small cups) but ready-made communion cups and items of domestic plate. With so much of the trade concentrated on this annual event, it is not surprising that Cambridge goldsmiths do not seem to have been as prosperous or as prominent as in other towns of similar size.

During the chalice conversion programme, one Norwich goldsmith, Thomas Buttell, moved to Cambridge, no doubt anticipating demand as attention turned to the Ely diocese. Thomas Buttell's mark is found on over thirty cups in Cambridgeshire, a typical example being the cup and cover of Willingham, dated 1569, which follows the Norwich form. In November 1568 the London company wardens visiting Stourbridge Fair found Buttell in possession of substandard communion cups and covers for which he was fined a total of 23s.[4] Christopher Buttell, who may be the same Christopher who is recorded as a journeyman working for the Ipswich goldsmith William Myles in 1557,[5] was probably a relation; his death is recorded in Cambridge in 1574.[6]

The Norwich goldsmith who used the mark IV over a heart, which has been variously attributed to Valentine Isborne and John Vanderpoest, supplied a cup and cover to St Andrew the Great in Cambridge. The cup is engraved *THIS FOR SENT TANDROS PARES IN KAMBREDGE*. It would seem most likely that the mark is Isborne's as the heart is probably a pun on his Christian name. It is unlikely, however, that Isborne moved to Cambridge like his colleague Buttell but instead had sold the cup and cover to the churchwardens at Stourbridge Fair: he is recorded in the Norwich Census of the Poor in 1570.[7]

Other goldsmiths working in Cambridge during the Elizabethan period were William Ramsey, George Wiscorne and James Welles. Only two goldsmiths seem to have been working in Cambridge in the early seventeenth century: a Mr Bradstone mentioned in 1622 and William Hayward, who in 1635 was paid 11s "moore than the 5 li and ould Cupp for the making of the New Challis" for Great St Mary's.[8]

Perhaps surprisingly, no plate in any Cambridge college can be identified as having been made locally. However, the three Esquire Bedells' staves of the University, which had been sent to Mr Blackwell in London in 1651 to have the royal arms replaced with those of the Commonwealth, were converted back to royalist pieces by Samuel Urlin, a Cambridge goldsmith, in 1663:

The old armes wt	1 oz 18 dwt	
at 5s the oz comes to		9s 6d
the new comes to silver chaseing and Gilding		
myne comes to more than the old one		2£ 6s —
the silver @ the new wtt	9 0	
the making		1 15 0
the Gilding		0 11 6
Received in full of this Bill		2 = 6 = 0
Samuel Urlin		
Witness John Houlden [9]		

No marks can be attributed to any Cambridge goldsmiths with the exception of Thomas Buttell, but marks of radiating stylized hearts similar to those found in the Waveney Valley are found on a few Elizabethan communion cups in the surrounding area, such as the one from Cheveley (now in the Fitzwilliam Museum), and could have been used by Cambridge goldsmiths.

1 Mary Bateson, ed., *Cambridge Guild Records*, Cambridge Antiquarian Society, Octavo Series 39, 1903.
2 "A Reconstruction of the Medieval Cambridge Market Place", *Proceedings of the Cambridge Antiquarian Society*, vol. 91, 2002, p. 84.
3 J. E. Foster, ed., *Churchwardens' Accounts of Great St Mary's, Cambridge: 1504-1635*, Cambridge Antiquarian Society, Octavo Series, 35, 1905, p. 94.
4 Barrett, *Norwich Silver*, p. 82.
5 Oman, *Church Plate*, p. 138.
6 Jackson, p. 342.
7 Barrett, *Norwich Silver*, p. 89; Barrett ascribed the mark IV over a heart to Isborne, but George Levine, writing in 1977, suggested Vanderpoest as a more likely candidate. He is listed in the 1570 Norwich subsidy list as "an alien" and his will, dated 1603, shows him, in contrast to Isborne and as one would expect of such an active producer of plate, to have been moderately wealthy and to have had dealings with several of the wealthiest "strangers" in the city (see Levine, "More Norwich Goldsmiths' Wills", p. 210).
8 Foster, p. 473.
9 Vouchers of University Accounts 1663, Cambridge University Archives U.Ac2(1); Mr Blackwell has recently been identified by Eric J. G. Smith as the goldsmith who used the hound sejant mark found on much of the best plate produced in the middle years of the seventeenth century; see E. J. G. Smith: "Richard Blackwell & Son" in *Silver Society Journal*, no. 15, 2003, pp. 19–45.

Church plate inventories in print

Cambridgeshire

Charles Oman lists a manuscript inventory done between 1893 and c. 1900 in the Library of the Cambridge Antiquarian Society, which he describes as "amateurish and unreliable".

Essex

Rev. G. Montagu Benton *et al*.: *Church Plate of the County of Essex*, London, 1926

Edwin Freshfield: *Church Plate in the Parish Churches of Essex*, part 1, Deaneries of Barking, Chafford (Romford) and Chelmsford (only part issued), London, 1899

Norfolk *(abbreviated as NA followed by name of the deanery)*

Norfolk inventories variously compiled by Rev. E. C. Hopper, Rev. C. R. Manning, Rev. H. S. Radcliffe or J. H. Walter in *Norfolk Archaeology*. Some were issued separately.

Deanery	volume	date	p.
Blofield	XX	1921	257
Beccles	XVI	1907	31
Brisley	XXIII	1929	19
Burnham	XXII	1926	133
Cranwich	XXIII	1929	221
Depwode	XV	1904	44
East Brooke	XVII	1907	153
add. note	XVI	1908	328
East and West Fincham	XXIV	1931	23
Elmham	XXII	1926	133
Fincham	XXIII	1929	233
Flegg	XIX	1917	185
Heacham	XXII	1926	260
Hingham Forehow	XVIII	1914	23
Holt	XXI	1926	37
Humbleyard	XVI	1907	240
add. note	XVII	1909	190
Loddon	XXIII	1929	45
Lynn	XVIII	1914	261
Lynn Borough	XXIV	1930	18
Lynn Marshland	XXIV	1934	270
Mitford	XVIII	1914	31
North Ingworth	XX	1921	150
Norwich	X	1888	65
Redenhall	IX	1884	68
Repps	XXI	1926	310
Rockland	XVII	1910	165
Sparham	XIX	1917	221
Taverham	XVI	1907	258
Thetford	XVI	1907	160

Deanery	volume	date	p.
Tunstead	XXII	1926	1
Walsingham	XX	1921	22
Waxham	XXI	1926	143
West Brooke	XVII	1910	263
Wisbech	XXIV	1934	285

Suffolk *(abbreviated as SCP followed by name of the deanery)*

Rev. E. C. Hopper *et al*.: "Church Plate in Suffolk" (Deaneries of Hoxne, Horningsheath, Thingoe, Hartismere, Wangford and the Colneys), *Suffolk Institute of Archaeology and Natural History*, 8, 1894, pp. 279–333

—: "Church Plate in Suffolk" (Deaneries of Clare, North and South Dunwich, Lavenham, Lothingland, Orford, South Elmham, Sudbury and Thedwastre, Bosmere, Carlford, Claydon, Ipswich, Loes, Samford, Hadleigh, Stow and Mildenhall, Blackburne, Thurlow and Wilford), *Suffolk Institute of Archaeology and Natural History*, 9, 1897, pp. 145–230, 279–306

Exhibitions

1902   *Art Loan*, Norwich, 1902
        Art Loan Exhibition, St Andrew's Hall, Norwich, 1902

1911   *Norwich Silver Plate*, Norwich, 1911
        *Loan Collections of Norwich Silver Plate (illustrated) and
        Paintings & Prints of Famous Norfolk Horses, Cattle &c. in
        the Norwich Castle Museum*, Norwich Castle Museum,
        Norwich, 1911

1929   *Park Lane*, London, 1929
        Loan Exhibition of Old English Plate, 25 Park Lane,
        London, 1929

1929   *Queen Charlotte's Loan*, London, 1929
        *Queen Charlotte's Loan Exhibition of Old Silver, English,
        Irish and Scottish*, Seaford House, London, 1929

1937   *How Exhibition*, London, 1937
        Exhibition (How of Edinburgh Ltd.), London, 1937

1955   *Antique Dealers' Fair,* London, 1955
        Antique Dealers' Fair and Exhibition, Grosvenor House,
        London, 1955

1958   *English Silver*, Ontario, 1958
        English Silver: Seven Centuries of English Domestic Silver,
        Royal Ontario Museum, Ontario, 1958

1961   *Church Treasures*, Blythburgh, 1961
        Suffolk Archdeaconry Exhibition of Church Treasures,
        Blythburgh Church, Blythburgh, Suffolk, 1961

1966   *Norwich Silver*, Norwich, 1966
        Norwich Silver 1565/1706, Norwich Castle Museum,
        Norwich, 1966

1967   *Church Treasures*, Ickworth, 1967
        Church Treasures of West Suffolk, Ickworth House,
        Horringer, Bury St Edmunds, Suffolk, 1967

1972   *Lynn Silver*, King's Lynn, 1972
        Lynn Silver, King's Lynn Museum & Art Gallery, King's
        Lynn, 1972

1973   *Medieval Art*, Norwich, 1973
        Medieval Art in East Anglia, 1300–1520, Norwich Castle
        Museum, Norwich, 1973

1977   *Grosvenor House Antiques Fair*, London, 1977
        Grosvenor House Antiques Fair, Grosvenor House,
        London, 1977

Abbreviations of sources cited

Alcorn
    Ellenor Alcorn, *English Silver in the Museum of Fine Arts, Boston*,
    vol. 1, Boston, 1993

Antique Dealers' Fair, London
    Antique Dealers' Fair, exh. cat., London, 1953

Ayres
    Brian Ayres, *Norwich A Fine City*, Stroud, 2003

Barrett, "Document"
    G. N. Barrett, "A Norwich Silver Document", *Norfolk
    Archaeology*, vol. 41, part 4, 1993, pp. 509–10

Barrett, "Haslewood Family"
    G. N. Barrett, "The Haslewood Family of Norwich", *Proceedings
    of the Society of Silver Collectors*, December 1960–June 1961; the
    same article, with minor revisions, appeared in *Norfolk
    Archaeology*, vol. 33, 1966, pp. 318–20

Barrett, *Norwich Silver*
    G. N. Barrett, *Norwich Silver and its Marks 1565–1702:
    The Goldsmiths of Norwich 1141–1750*, Norwich, 1981

Barrett, "Problem Solved"
    G. N. Barrett, "A 'Norwich Silver' Problem Solved?" *Norfolk
    Archaeology*, vol. 39, part 3, 1986, pp. 313–4

Barry and Brooks
    J. Barry and C. Brooks, *The Middling Sort of People: Culture,
    Society and Politics in England 1550–1800*, Basingstoke, 1994

Beecheno, *St Andrew's Church*
    F. R. Beecheno, *Notes on the Church of St Andrew, Norwich*,
    Norwich, 1883

Beecheno, *St Andrew's Parish*
    F. R. Beecheno, *St Andrew's Church and Parish*, Norwich, 1888

Best
    D. Best, "The Bungay Navigation", *Norfolk Industrial
    Archaeology Society Journal*, 2003

Blomefeld
    Francis Blomefield, completed by Charles Parkin, *An Essay
    Towards a Topographical History of the County of Norfolk*, 2nd
    edn., London, 1805–10

Butler
    Robin Butler, *The Albert Collection: Five Hundred Years of British
    and European Silver*, London, 2004

Casley
    Henry C. Casley, "An Ipswich worker of Elizabethan church
    plate", *Proceedings of the Suffolk Institute of Archaeology and
    Natural History*, vol. 12, 1904, pp. 169–83

Church Treasures, *Blythburgh*
    Suffolk Archdeaconry Exhibition of Church Treasures (exh. cat.),
    Blythburgh Church, 1961

Church Treasures, *Ickworth*
    Church Treasures of West Suffolk (exh. cat.), The National Trust, Ickworth, Horringer, 1967

Clayton, *Dictionary*
    Michael Clayton, *The Collector's Dictionary of the Silver and Gold of Great Britain and North America*, rev. edn., London, 1985

Clayton, *History*
    Michael Clayton, *The Christie's Pictorial History of English and American Silver*, Oxford, 1985

Clifford, *Oxford*
    Helen M. Clifford, *A Treasured Inheritance: 600 Years of Oxford College Silver* (exh. cat.), Oxford, 2004

Cox
    J. Charles Cox, *Churchwardens' Accounts from the Fourteenth Century to the Close of the Seventeenth Century*, London, 1894

Cripps
    Wilfred Cripps, *Old English Plate*, London, 1901

de Jong and de Groot
    Marijnke de Jong & I. de Groot, *Ornamentprenten in het Rijksprentenkabinet*, vol. 1, *15de–16de Eeuw*, Rijksmuseum, Amsterdam, 1988

Dymond
    David Dymond, *The Norfolk Landscape*, 2nd edn., London, 1990

Emmerson
    Robin Emmerson (ed.), *Norwich Silver in the Collection of Norwich Castle Museum*, Norwich, 1981

English Silver, Ontario
    English Silver: Seven Centuries of English Domestic Silver, Royal Ontario Museum (exh. cat.), Ontario, 1958

Evans
    J. T. Evans, *17th Century Norwich: Politics, Religion and Government 1620–1690*, Oxford, 1979

Frederiks
    J. W. Frederiks, *Dutch Silver*, vol. 3, *Wrought Plate of the Central, Northern and Southern Provinces from the Renaissance until the End of the Eighteenth Century*, The Hague, 1960

Freemen, Lynn
    A Calendar of the Freemen of Lynn 1292–1836, Norwich, 1913

Freemen, Norwich
    Percy Millican (ed.), *The Register of the Freemen of Norwich 1548–1713*, Norwich, 1934

Freemen, Yarmouth
    A Calendar of the Freemen of Yarmouth 1429–1800, Norwich, 1910

Glanville, *Tudor and Early Stuart*
    Philippa Glanville, *Silver in Tudor and Early Stuart England*, London, 1990

Glanville and Goldsborough
    Philippa Glanville & Jennifer Faulds Goldsborough, *Women Silversmiths 1685–1845: Works from the Collection of the National Museum of Women in the Arts*, Washington D.C., 1990

Granville Baker
    B. Granville Baker, *Waveney*, London, 1924

Griffiths and Smith
    Elizabeth Griffiths and Hassell Smith, *"Buxom to the Mayor": A History of the Norwich Freemen and the Town Close Estate*, Norwich, 1987

Grimwade
    A. G. Grimwade, *London Goldsmiths 1697–1837, Their Marks and Lives*, rev. edn., London, 1990

Grosvenor House Antiques Fair, London
    Grosvenor House Antiques Fair (exh. cat.), London, 1977

Gruber
    Alain Gruber (ed.), *The History of Decorative Arts: The Renaissance and Mannerism in Europe*, New York, 1994

Hartop, *Fogg*
    Christopher Hartop, *British and Irish Silver in the Fogg Museum, Harvard University*, Cambridge, Mass., forthcoming

Hartop, *Huguenot Legacy*
    Christopher Hartop, *The Huguenot Legacy: English Silver 1680–1760, from the Alan and Simone Hartman Collection*, London, 1996

Hartop, *Norwich Goldsmiths*
    Christopher Hartop, *Norwich Goldsmiths of the Elizabethan Period*, dissertation, University of Bristol, 1980

Hawker, "Makers"
    Rev. P. Hawker, "Lincolnshire makers of church plate", *Silver Society Journal*, 1999, pp. 185–7

Hawker, "Treasury"
    Rev. P. Hawker, "The Lincoln Cathedral Treasury of Diocesan Plate", *Proceedings of the Society of Silver Collectors*, vol. 1, no. 1, 1961–2, pp. 8–12

Heal
    Heal, *The London Goldsmiths 1200–1800*, Newton Abbott, 1972

Holland
    Margaret Holland, *Old Country Silver*, Newton Abbott, 1971

How, "Criticisms"
    G. E. P. How, "Norwich silver. Some constructive criticisms on errors of ascription", *Apollo*, vol. 40, December, 1944

How, *Ellis Catalogue*
    G. E. P. How, *Catalogue of a Remarkable Collection of 16th and 17th Century Provincial Silver Spoons Incorporating the Entire Collection Left by the Late H. D. Ellis, Esq. at His Death, the Property of Lieut.-Col. I. Benett-Stanford*, Sotheby's, London, November 13–14, 1935

How, *Exhibition*
How of Edinburgh Ltd., *Exhibition* (exh. cat.), London, 1937

How, *Spoons*
G. E. P. and J. P. How, *English and Scottish Silver Spoons*, 3 vols., London, vol. 1, 1952; vol. 2, 1953; vol. 3, 1957

Hudson and Tingey
Hudson & Tingey, *Selected Records of the City of Norwich*, Norwich, 1923

Inglis, "Gilbert"
Brand Inglis, "An ostrich egg cup by Lawrence Gilbert of Colchester", *Silver Society Journal*, autumn 1997, pp. 570–72

Inglis, "The King's Lynn goldsmiths"
Brand Inglis, "The King's Lynn goldsmiths", *Proceedings of the Silver Society*, vol. 2 , part 7, 1972, pp. 46–52

Jackson
Sir Charles Jackson, *English Goldsmiths and Their Marks*, rev. edn., Woodbridge, 1989, with chapter on East Anglia by Geoffrey Barrett

Jackson, *English Plate*
Sir Charles Jackson, *An Illustrated History of English Plate*, London, 1911

Kent, *Somerset Silver*
Timothy Kent, *Seventeenth Century Somerset Silver: Spoones & Gobletts*, Taunton, 2004

Kent, *West Country Silver Spoons*
Timothy Kent, *West Country Silver Spoons and Their Makers 1550–1750*, London, 1992

Ketton-Cremer
R. W. Ketton-Cremer, *Norfolk in the Civil War*, London, 1968

Kirkpatrick
John Kirkpatrick (ed. Rev. W Hudson), *The Streets and Lanes of the City of Norwich*, Norfolk and Norwich Archaeological Society, Norwich, 1889

L'Estrange and Rye
John L'Estrange and William Rye, *Calendar of the Freemen of Norwich, 1317–1603*, London, 1888

Lever
Christopher Lever, *Goldsmiths and Silversmiths of England*, London, 1975

Levine
G. Levine, "Norwich Goldsmiths' Marks", *Norfolk Archaeology*, vol. 34, part 3, 1968, pp. 293–302

Levine, "More Norwich Goldsmiths' Wills"
G. Levine, "More Norwich Goldsmiths' Wills", *Norfolk Archaeology*, vol. 37, part 2, 1979, pp. 208–13

Levine, "Norwich Goldsmiths' Wills"
G. Levine, "Some Norwich Goldsmiths' Wills", *Norfolk Archaeology*, vol. 35, part 4, 1973, pp. 483–90

Lynn Silver, King's Lynn
James Gilchrist and Brand Inglis, *Lynn Silver* (exh. cat.), 1972

MacCulloch
Diarmaid MacCulloch, *Suffolk and the Tudors: Politics and Religion in an English County 1500–1600*, Oxford, 1986

Mann
E. Mann, *Old Bungay*, London, 1934

Medieval Art, Norwich
P. Lasko and N. J. Morgan (eds.), *Medieval Art in East Anglia, 1300–1520* (exh. cat.), Norwich, 1973

Moffatt
Harold Charles Moffatt, *Old Oxford Plate*, Oxford, 1906

Moore
Andrew Moore, "The Norwich School of Artists & The New Medium of Photography" in *A Period Eye: Photography Then & Now*, Richard Denyer & Andrew Moore (eds.), vol. 1, Norwich, 2003

Norwich Silver, Norwich
Sheena Smith, ed., *Norwich Silver 1565/1706* (exh. cat.), Norwich, 1966

Norwich Silver Plate, Norwich
Catalogue of Loan Collections of Norwich Silver Plate (illustrated) and Paintings & Prints of Famous Norfolk Horses, Cattle &c. in the Norwich Castle Museum (exh. cat.), Norwich, 1911

NRS
Proceedings of the Norfolk Record Society, Norwich

Oman
Charles Oman, *English Silversmiths' Work Civil and Domestic: an Introduction*, London, 1965

Oman, *Church Plate*
Charles Oman, *English Church Plate*, London, 1957

Oman, "Civic Plate"
Charles Oman, "The Civic Plate and Insignia of the City of Norwich", *The Connoisseur*, vol. 155, 1964, pp. 229–35; vol. 156, 1964, pp. 6–9

Oman, "Norwich Silversmiths"
Charles Oman, "Art of the Norwich Silversmiths", *Country Life*, April 28, 1966, pp. 1020–1

Park Lane, London
Loan Exhibition of Old English Plate, 25 Park Lane (exh. cat.), London, 1929

Pevsner
The Buildings of England, North-East Norfolk and Norwich, Nikolaus Pevsner, London, 1962

Pierce Gould
R. Pierce Gould, "The Laws of the Goldsmiths of Norwich, 1624", *Norfolk Archaeology*, vol. 29, 1946, pp. 211–21

Queen Charlotte's Loan, London
W. W. Watts, *Queen Charlotte's Loan Exhibition of Old Silver, English, Irish and Scottish* (exh. cat.), London, 1929

Reynolds and Machlachlan
G. D. Reynolds & P. Machlachlan, *Guide to Heraldry in Suffolk Churches*, Suffolk Heraldry Society, 1990

Rye, Court Books
W. Rye, *Extracts from the Court Books of the City of Norwich*, Norwich, 1905

Scarfe
Norman Scarfe, *The Suffolk Landscape*, London, 1972

Schofield
R. S. Schofield, "The Geographical Distribution of Wealth in England 1334 to 1649", *Economic History Review*, 18, 1965, pp. 483–510

Seaby
B. A. Seaby, *Standard Catalogue of British Coins*, London, 1970

Skottowe
Phillip F. Skottowe, *The Leaf and the Tree, The Story of an English Family*, London, 1963

Statham
M. Statham, *The Book of Bury St Edmunds*, Buckingham, 1988

Sympson
E. Mansel Sympson, "Notes on Lincolnshire church plate", *Proceedings of the Society of Antiquaries*, 2nd series, vol. 22, 1908, pp. 1–7

ter Molen
J. R. ter Molen, *Zilver: Catalogus van de voorwerpen van edelmetaal in de collectie van het Museum Boymans-van Beunigen*, Rotterdam, 1994

Wake
Thomas Wake, "Silver by Norwich Craftsmen", *Apollo*, vol. 39, August 1944, pp. 40–41 and vol. 40, September 1944, pp. 60–66

White
White, *White's Directory of Suffolk*, Sheffield, 1844

Index of marks

Page numbers are shown in roman type and those for illustrations are shown in italic. Catalogue numbers are shown in boldface type.

Index

Page numbers are shown in roman type and those for illustrations are shown in italic. Catalogue numbers are shown in boldface type.

Photographic credits
The photographs, unless otherwise credited, were taken by GGS Creative Graphics Norwich. Those credited to the Worshipful Company of Goldsmiths were taken by A. A. Barnes; those of nos. 26 and 95 by Clarissa Bruce. The photographs of nos. 13, 21–2, 45, 54–6, 60 and 93 were supplied by the lenders of these items.